Business, Media,
and the Law

Business, Media, and the Law
The Troubled Confluence

ROBERT LAMB
WILLIAM G. ARMSTRONG, JR.
KAROLYN R. MORIGI

NEW YORK UNIVERSITY PRESS · New York *and* London

Copyright © 1980 by New York University

Library of Congress Cataloging in Publication Data

Lamb, Robert, 1941 (June 19)-
   Business, media, and the law.

   Bibliography: p.
   Includes index.
   1. Corporation law—United States.   2. Trade
regulation—United States.   3. Disclosure of
information (Securities law)—United States.
4. Mass media and business—United States.
I. Armstrong, William George, 1947 (Dec. 16)-
joint author.   II. Morigi, Karolyn R., joint author, 1954 (May 11)
III. Title.
KF1416.L35   346.73′066   78-55569
ISBN 0-8147-0565-0

Manufactured in the United States of America

Acknowledgments

The support and generosity of many individuals and several organizations made this book possible. Originally, this project was inspired by Dr. William R. Dill, Dean of the Graduate School of Business Administration at New York University, for whom we all once worked. Dean Dill enlisted the support of the International Paper Foundation, part of whose grant to New York University funded our research. Lee Foster, president of the foundation, expressed continuing personal interest in our progress. We were also heartened by the personal encouragement of Stan Smith, chairman of International Paper Company, one of the few corporate chairmen in the country who rose to the top after first serving as his company's public relations director.

We gathered material for this book through months of reading journals, studies, and discussing the various aspects of the issues with practitioners. In addition, we conducted a two-day conference on business and press relations with some prominent individuals in both fields. In searching for an appropriate cosponsor for the conference we discovered George Mair and Jack Cox, of the Foundation for American Communications (FACS). FACS, which runs conferences for business and civic organizations, made its New York City debut by running our conference at the St. Regis Sheraton Hotel in September 1978.

Material from previous FACS conferences, and the overall ability of FACS personnel to put together a first-rate meeting, contributed substantially to our research. FACS also attracted support from the Public Relations Society of America, Northeast Chapter.

From NYU's distinguished faculty, we received thoughtul insight and cooperation. Special thanks for their personal participation go to Irving Kristol; Barbara Coe and William Guth of the business faculty; Norman Redlich and Homer Kripke of the law faculty; and David Rubin and John Kochevar of the journalism faculty. Among the outstanding alumni

v

we tapped, special gratitude goes to Lewis H. Young, editor of Business Week. We must also mention the team at NYU Press: Publisher Malcolm Johnson, Editor Robert Bull, and Despina Papazoglou. Al Kingon and Thomas Rosenbaum provided valuable help for the finished product. Chuck Silberstein helped in the early stages of research. Debora Nikosey helped us in so many ways that it would be difficult to list everything.

As in any such project, there are very personal thanks to be made to those whose support behind the scenes was essential: NL, PLM and MDM, R and C. These people and many others invested in our enterprise. If our product is worthwhile, it is largely because we listened to their advice.

Robert Lamb
William G. Armstrong Jr.
Karolyn R. Morigi

New York, New York, April 1980

Contents

Introduction

The decade of the seventies witnessed a fierce conflict between three major institutions in the United States: business, media, and government. Each is at fault and bears some responsibility. John deButts, former chairman of AT&T, admitted the failings of business to President Gerald Ford and Ben Bradlee, Editor of *The Washington Post:*

> What we need is more open, frank discussion between the media and government and business. John Chancellor told me once "if we've got a controversial subject to put on the air, I can make one telephone call and get a consumerist. I can make one more call and get a labor leader, and I can make a half a dozen and not get a businessman who is willing to come in here." To me that is a terrible, terrible mistake.

Every society is dependent upon the development and maintenance of confidence and mutual understanding on the part of its principal members to assure continuance. American society of the last decade experienced the painful erosion of fundamental elements of such confidence and understanding.

Public confidence in all three of the institutions decreased drastically. In a world of image-makers, perceptions became the new reality. Vietnam, Watergate, Koreagate, and other corporate, political, and journalistic abuses raised questions about the integrity not only of the individual participants, but about the very institutions themselves. As a result, the public is questioning, as never before, the right of business to control production and the authority of government to collect taxes and make laws. Some ponder the media's awesome power to control news and disseminate information loosening the fiber of American institutions. In total, it is a confidence war. Each institution tries to score points and strengthen its own credibility by playing on the weaknesses of its adversaries. At the same time, the battleground has been changed dramatically, and business has failed to respond to the change.

Today, the doors to corporate board rooms are being pried open, and business is being forced to disclose information once considered proprietary.

> The difference in this generation of businesss leaders and journalists is that business is a legitimate news story now, and it wasn't 25 years ago. I think business operated in a comparative vacuum. Certainly the government wasn't looking over your shoulders then as now, and now you've got journalists.
>
> Ben Bradlee,
> Editor, *The Washington Post*

> At the same time that society is asking corporations for more disclosure, we find that companies are becoming more reluctant to disclose matters. The cop-out that you hear quite often is: "We don't want to talk to the press, because they're only going to screw it up." If you don't talk to us, we may screw it up even worse. And it seems to me that it is a mistake for any corporation not to try to get its viewpoint out to the public on a subject that the press thinks is going to interest the public.
>
> Lewis Young,
> Editor-in-Chief, *Business Week*

If not corrected, the adversarial relationship that has developed among the media and corporations and the government will have severe repercussions. While journalists and regulators routinely dissect corporate executives and politicians for evidence of payoffs, mismanagement, and secret deals, business executives just as routinely excoriate journalists and regulators for ignorance of business and economics, for distorting facts and misinforming the public.

Many leaders of business enterprises are suspicious of journalists and ignorant of media operations. The media have the same attitude. They think business is unresponsive, and therefore guilty of something, myopic and reactionary.

> My feelings about business were shaped by an incident which occurred at the Detroit Economic Club in 1960 when I was there representing Newsweek Magazine, and I was covering the cam-

paign. The audience was composed of only vice presidents of General Motors, and they cornered me and tried to get me to predict who was going to win that election. I begged off, but they insisted. Finally, I said very quietly that I thought maybe Jack Kennedy would win. After the session, a stubby little vice president of General Motors came up to me and he pushed his stubby little finger into my chest and said, "Sonny, if you want to amount to a hill of (deleted) in your business, stick close to Dick Nixon." . . . Which, of course, is exactly what I did.

Ben Bradlee

Under Justice Brandeis' creed that "sunlight is the best disinfectant," the press has taken a fresh interest in business and has begun to probe into product safety, directorships, financing and business ethics. Moreover, business reporting is no longer the step-child of American journalism.

While business has come under increasing scrutiny and more disclosure is being demanded, the media industry has been changing dramatically. A communications revolution has been under way, and the industry is experiencing a metamorphosis in technology and in emphasis.

Gallup found that high school students estimated that the average profit of an American business on a dollar of sales was 30 cents. College students estimated that it was 45 cents. And of course, it's a little better than a nickel. Where would students get ideas like that? They aren't taught it at home. They aren't really taught it in high school even though there might be an anti-business bias in some pedagogical institutions. They're not really taught things like that. They don't read the business pages of newspapers. The average student, when he graduates from high school, has spent 12,000 hours in the classroom and 25,000 hours before a television set. So you have to assume that the misconception stems from the way in which they are informed.

Frank Shakespeare,
President, RKO General

The spotlight that for many years was reserved for political and sports figures has been turned on business. Government has initiated some of this probing, and intense investigation by various media has facilitated more of it. The enhanced attraction of journalism as a profession and the profusion of media outlets, particularly the tremendous growth in broadcast media and the changing technology of the print media, are factors which have alerted business that its public posture must change. The relationship between the government and business, therefore, has changed too. Not only is there a demand for the government to protect investors, but there is a clamoring for government regulation in all aspects of business, including hiring policies, advertising, product content, mergers, acquisitions, investments, and composition of boards of directors.

American business has succeeded so far in spite of what many executives regard as direct opposition, intimidation, and conflicting directives from the federal government. Government at all levels has constrained economic growth, often regardless of whether constraints and changes are efficient or productive.

> The Federal Government alone takes virtually half of business' profits, binds it with red tape, snows it with paper work, investigates and regulates and legislates it beyond all reason.
>   John W. Hill,
>   Chairman of the
>   Executive Committee and Founder,
>   Hill and Knowlton, Inc.

In summary, business executives, journalists, and regulators each demonstrate a lack of understanding of each others' professions: neglect for attaining basic comprehension of the roles, routines, objectives, and constraints the other institutions face in our increasingly compartmentalized and complex society. The result is a lack of meaningful dialogue.

For business, there are two important issues. First, the role of companies, even private companies, is changing, and the level of public involvement in company affairs is increasing. Executives and directors have to think now of "stakeholders" and not merely stockholders.

Second, the rules of the game have changed rapidly, and are continuing to do so. Government and the media invoke the name of "the people" and demand that business disclose more of its transactions, policies, and practices. Such demands from the media and from special interest groups are considerably more sophisticated than they were only a decade or two ago: unit pricing on groceries, labels on clothing, recalls on defective automobiles and appliances, financial data about pension funds, a clamoring for public participation in the very governance of corporations.

Unfortunately too many people in business want us to be not a microscope, but a megaphone for business.

Tom Brokaw,
NBC news correspondent

Media and government were once thought to be advocates of the free enterprise system and, therefore, allies of business firms. However, public acceptance no longer comes easily or cheaply, especially for big business. The new environment of business requires that exeutives accept their public responsibilities and the need for effective public relations and corporate communications.

You cannot do that job of public relations for a company or stockholders, et cetera, without a little preparation, a little education and a little competition. I happen to think what (business representatives) do in communicating (their) position is very important in our society. But they better do a better job because what I read sometimes isn't as good as it ought to be.

Gerald Ford,
Former President of the United States

This book is an attempt to relax the tension that has been generated from the adversarial posture of business, media, and government. We hope this analysis will break down some of the barriers and explain to practitioners and students of law, media, and business what are the issues, misunderstandings, and solutions. It is designed to aid upper and middle management in assessing corporate disclosure requirements and personal communications techniques.

Our work has grown out of lengthy research and several conferences held around the country, including a two-day conference on business-media relations in September 1978, cosponsored by The New York University Graduate School of Business Administration and the Foundation for American Communications. We have drawn widely from all the published material in this field, and the most analytical and perceptive ideas, examples and recommendations. We believe this is the first comprehensive survey of the contention between these three important institutions.

PART I

CHAPTER 1

A Rebuttal to Public Skepticism

The decade of the 1970s will be known as the decade that the American public lost faith in big business. The number of those agreeing that "business tries to strike a balance between profits and the interests of the public" dropped from 70 percent in 1968 to 15 percent by the end of the 1970s, according to pollster Daniel Yankelovich.[1] During roughly the same period, polls taken by Louis Harris indicated that those who express "a great deal of confidence in the people in charge of running major companies" dropped from 55 to 18 percent.[2] By way of contrast, the public felt differently about small business. Asked to rank 20 institutions for honesty, dependability, and integrity, Americans ranked small business second only to banks—even ahead of organized religion. Big business was ranked far down the list, ahead of only ad agencies, the two political parties, labor leaders, and politicians.

With cynicism and skepticism running rampant, business is finding that it must be able to accommodate its goals and programs to the interests of external constituencies with the same skill and determination that many companies have acquired in dealing with workers, lower levels of management, stockholders, and financial analysts.

FACELESS LEADERS

In the early 1970s, Ralph Nader wrote about "hidden executives." These were nameless and faceless people who made important decisions behind closed doors. Although the atmosphere had begun to change by the end of the decade, the public still had difficulty naming the leaders and main spokesmen of the American business community. Beyond the obvious top few names, a Ford, a Rockefeller, a DuPont, most people would be hard pressed to name the leaders of the nation's largest firms. By contrast, many would likely have little difficulty in naming prominent

3

figures in each of several sports. We know the names of the top golf pros, the best major league ball players, the best running backs, coaches, and so on. Leading entertainers and politicians enjoy equal familiarity. Even the names and faces of local media personalities are more easily recognized than corporate brass. Business leaders have shielded themselves from public view, partly by design. By remaining out of the limelight, they avoid the notoriety, the physical dangers that exposure can bring, the loss of personal privacy, the sharpshooting press, and what many regard as vulgar exhibitionism. Many avoid the limelight because they fear committing verbal stumbles or mistakes in public, possibly in front of millions of people watching television.

Sandy Socolow, executive producer of the "CBS Evening News," has lamented his own difficulty in finding industry spokesmen to appear, especially when a particularly "messy or unfortunate" situation occurs. After years of such frustration, he has come to the conclusion that business executives do not want news coverage. In frustration, he issued a challenge to business: "You people would be perfectly satisfied if we did nothing but report statistics—cost of living, stock market, indexes. I submit that you guys don't really want more business reporting in the way I think of reporting business." [3]

Socolow commented later: "It's one hell of a tough job to get a businessman to appear on live broadcasts. When we finally managed to get the chairman of the board of General Motors [on 'Face the Nation'], he was happy as a clam when it was all over. He found out it didn't hurt one bit."

Nameless and faceless individuals, however, will never generate public support, and without public support, business cannot hope to survive, much less beat back restrictive legislation or receive fair treatment in the press. Only the efforts of recognizable personalities can bring this about.

One of the requirements of strength and leadership that modern democracy has come to demand of political leaders is effective communication and open disclosure.

REMEDIES RUNNING RAMPANT

Some of the suggestions and remedies for redressing skepticism are novel; some are thoughtful and natural outgrowths of the new business environment; others are thoroughly frightening and potentially destructive of the system as we know it. Some of the proposals are from the far left:

- Business should be forced to disclose all of its transactions.
- Business should be chartered by the federal, not state, government.
- Business should be taxed whenever profits exceed a certain percentage because profits represent consumers' overpayment.

Some are from the far right:

- Business should stop doing business with the federal government until the government puts its own house in order.
- Business should cease funding universities that hire professors with antibusiness biases,

Others are more moderate:

- Business should make a voluntary effort to inform the public about the pressures under which it operates.
- Business executives should take a more active, more public role in the debate and management of public affairs.

THE ERA OF PUBLIC ENTERPRISE

Until 1976, there was ever-increasing pressure put upon business to disclose more of its dealings to the government.

The energy industry, for example, came under particularly harsh public criticism due to a variety of international and domestic political developments, including tax laws written during the previous two decades which encouraged the exportation of drilling and refining capacity, the embargo by OPEC (the Organization of Petroleum Exporting Countries) in 1973, and the disruption in oil supply following the Iranian revolution of 1979. During that period, the energy companies were caught taking advantage of public and governmental confusion. The oil companies sustained the brunt of the blame for the energy crisis, and many people held the companies responsible for fabricating crisis after crisis to drive up prices.

Few of the oilmen have been willing to stand up and talk back to the government publicly or to take their complicated lessons in economics, world politics, and the energy business directly to the people. One prominent exception was Mobil Oil. The company undertook a pugnacious defense of the energy industry through a series of large display ads opposite the editorial page of many American newspapers. In those ads, the firm forged not only a case for its own survival—which was threatened by Congress—but also developed a new method for responding to government pressure and pointing up conflicting government statements and actions. Mobil actually ushered in a new era for corporate advertising, now known as "advocacy advertising," as a result of this campaign.

Another version of such a public campaign was undertaken by Republic Steel, which faced hostility over environmental actions. The company launched an advertising program describing its financial interdependence with the cities in which its plants were located. Each commercial ended with the suggestion, "You probably have some Republic Steel money in your pocket right now."

Sears Roebuck & Company, the nation's largest retailer, had long been embroiled in a dispute with the government over employment and hiring practices. Although there had been very few findings of actual wrongdoing on the part of the company, the argument had resulted in much adverse publicity. In frustration over the case, the company finally refused to conduct business with the government until the matter was resolved. The decision cost Sears more than $20 million a year, but it underscored its contention that the government should stay out of its affairs.

The three examples given above also illustrate that some businesses have been willing to strike back at what they consider unjustified government intervention. However, for the most part, American business executives have been loathe to take on their adversaries in public—nor have they had the stomach or the skill for such encounters. Often, they preferred to ignore political pressures, confident that their company would outlast any administration or political leader. That attitude prevailed in Cleveland, where big business was the target of an unrelenting campaign of rebuke by the mayor. Therefore, the business community there consistently lost referenda affecting its interests. As Cleveland became the second major city to endure a financial default (after the New York City default on its Municipal Notes in 1975), some of the large firms headquartered there, notably Addressograph-Multigraph, Harris Corp., White Motors, and Diamond Shamrock, moved their operations to other cities.

Difficulties and misunderstandings need never escalate to such dramatic levels, however. Numerous avenues of action exist within the framework of the law and good taste. Broadly, such actions involve changing the government leaders, influencing public leaders, and appealing through the media for public support. All such activities, properly executed, may result in a more favorable climate in which to do business, and each has been tried with varying degrees of success.

CHANGING GOVERNMENT LEADERS:
POLITICAL ACTION COMMITTEES

The campaign finance law of 1976 permitted the creation of corporate political-action committees, which enabled companies to take up voluntary collections from their employees and to donate those funds to political candidates or committes. (It is illegal for the funds to come from the companies' earnings—they must derive from employees' donations.) This type of activity can have considerable impact upon who gets elected. Since 1976, these committees have become the fastest-growing source of American campaign financing. The growth of corporate PACs, to almost 900 by 1980, has meant a shift toward supporting Republican candidates. In a recent Congressional election, corporate donors gave 61 percent of their contributions to Republicans and 39 percent to Democrats.[4]

The development of corporate political action committees suggests a sharpening of political consciousness within the business community; it reflects the enlargement of concern with public affairs that goes beyond traditional public relations. It indicates a new awareness, outside as well as within the business world, of business' role in the socio-political system. Business' heightened involvement in this aspect of the political process should, at the very least, clarify the dialog with its critics.

Another political technique adopted by some business concerns involves permitting executives a leave of one or two years to serve in public office. Executive loan programs, such as the arrangement by which Felix Rohatyn of Lazard Frères headed the New York Municipal Assistance Corporation (M.A.C.), functioned well during New York City's financial crisis; but a number of reservations have been expressed, primarily over possible conflicts of interest. Such sharing of expertise might benefit the firm lending its executive as well as the public whom the executive is serving. Many modern firms now permit such political involvement by their employees, although others traditionally look to employees only for production and results related directly to the business.

INFLUENCING PUBLIC LEADERS

It is striking how few business leaders actually know on a first-name basis the government officials and regulators whose decisions affect the vitality of their firms. For years, business leaders had been unwilling to meet and brief decision-makers in Washington and the state capitals and, if not to try outright to get them to adopt a certain position, at least to get them to understand the constraints under which they were operating. Labor, for decades, operated a very successful lobbying effort, but only in recent years has business begun to make a similar effort. Recently, for example, the Business Roundtable was begun in Washington at which top government leaders and regulators meet with industry leaders. Such meetings also have taken place outside of the public arena, where quieter, more rational approaches to problem-solving can be taken and where "posturing" by the political leaders is unnecessary. Unfortunately, some political leaders still do not wish to hear the views of business community representatives, and public interest groups such as Common Cause insist upon making public the logs of all government executives.

The formal, legal mechanisms of lobbying have taken on new importance during the past decade. The decline of the Congressional seniority system has meant that there is less likelihood of influencing legislation by "getting to" *one* representative. The Congressional power system is now so diversified that the efforts of lobbyists are required to approach a large number of Congressmen and government agencies. Corporations, therefore, have increased their Washington staffs and budgets. The Ford Motor Company, for example, had three lobbyists in the 1960s; it now has more than 40. *Time* magazine estimates that lobbyists now spend $1 billion per year to influence opinion in Washington, plus another billion on public opinion across the nation.[5]

Among their activities, lobbyists go so far as to write many of the bills introduced in Congress. They also pass along drafts of legislation, talking points, or whole speeches to the members. Many Congressmen welcome such research and writing because the demands on Congressmen's time are so great that it may well be impossible to be expert in each one of the many subjects on which they must speak and vote. The lobbyists, however, can explore in detail the elements of an issue of concern to their company or industry. A corporate lobbyist must also inform his company and its managers about what is coming up in Congress or in the various agencies. With federal spending approaching $600 billion per year, lobbyists also must try to obtain or redirect funds for their company. Thus, agricultural lobbyists, for example, push for farm price supports; lobbyists for Lockheed, Penn Central and Chrysler for government bailouts; steel companies for trigger price mechanisms to prevent dumping of lower-cost imported steel. Each of these intense efforts points up the kind of interest that corporations and whole industries undertake to protect themselves by trying to influence legislation.

Business has scored some notable victories in recent years as a result of lobbying, so much so that some business leaders have advised caution. "In the heady atmosphere of recent public policy successes, the temptation to excess could, in the long term, create an antibusiness backlash of dangerous dimensions, just as the demonstrably excessive demands of some unions have already weakened the political clout of organized labor," says William S. Sneath, chairman of Union Carbide.

Sneath and his colleagues recommend that perhaps business should try to influence public leaders not only by lobbying, but also through the more circuitous route of public pressure: "Our by-lines appear on the op-ed pages side by side with those of our critics. We take students to lunch and we take our critics to task. We are even learning to take journalists into our confidence." [6] One leading energy company, following Sneath's advice, recently hired an individual to coordinate not only the firm's political action committee and a portion of its public affairs program, but also to set up a network of 300 managers around the country to meet and work with local and state political leaders, coordinate letter-writing campaigns favoring the company's positions as well as writing letters to the editors, and organizing a speakers bureau. The same firm has as one of its goals the overturning of the political majority in one state legislature whose decisions are crucial to the firm's interest.

While all this political expertise and maneuvering may ultimately be useful, warning signals have been raised by some executives.

Sneath also has warned against mistaking the tactics and the techniques of public influence for the real source of ultimate public influence: public trust. "Business may complain about misguided environmental regulation, but the message the public too often hears is that we want the right, carte blanche, to pollute lakes and rivers. When we cross swords with OSHA [Occupational Safety and Health Administration), the appearance is that business cares less about worker health than about profits."

Sneath offers six rules for business leaders to follow in order to gain public trust.

- Since the role of money in politics will always be suspect, it is important to be careful about the relative benefits and hazards of even legitimate contributions. There is certainly good reason to support politicians who are willing to hear your side of an issue, but there is also good reason to shun any dealings with those whose votes are for sale.
- Gaining a reputation for integrity is the surest way to become a

respected part of the policy-making process. In testimony and policy statements, stick to the facts and to reasonable, credible interpretations of them.

- Know when to get involved and when *not* to. Stick to policy issues that affect business directly. Be very circumspect about heavy spending on issues in which there is no clear-cut corporate interest.
- Avoid all appearances of coercing people in or out of government, including employees and plant communities. If financial resources are used to do this, the result might be failure.
- Remember that, when you have done all the effective communicating and lobbying one could reasonably expect on an issue, and still have not convinced people, then it may be time to back off.
- Total victory and total defeat are equally rare in a democracy; the American system works best by balancing interests—not by aggravating differences.

APPEALING TO THE PUBLIC

Ultimately, the case for business must be carried directly to the public. But this has frightened most business executives in the past, for it is in the public arena where the most skill in communicating is required. A slip of the tongue, for example, can send stock prices tumbling. In addition, the print and broadcast media are seen as hostile territory for many in business. The press for too long has been seen (and has seen itself) as the adversary of business. The press seems only to discuss business when something goes wrong. Fortunately, some firms and consultants are beginning to engage in what FACS (Foundation for American Communications) calls "precrisis planning," the deliberate preparation and opening of lines of communication before disaster strikes. (Precrisis planning will be considered later in this volume.)

Business continuously struggles to arrive at an appropriate allocation of management's time. Today, one of the highest priorities involves skill in communicating to external publics. More and more, management is likely to seek advice on how to dress for television, how to respond on camera, or to enroll in diction lessons. Consulting firms such as Communispond and others extract an exobitant fee for training executives in these areas, and management willingly pays.

Not long ago, those moving up the executive ladder sought to master the intricacies of operations and organizational structure of the firm they would manage, but the modern executive may find when he gets to the top that his role is turned inside out. He may well spend over half his time in sessions with outsiders: government regulators, security analysts, legislators, trade associations, consumers, other public groups, and the news media. As a result, top managers are being called upon to take the initiative in the areas of public policy. It is the exercise of such influence and public leadership which can produce the most satisfactory results for business as well as for its presumed nemesis, the news media.

The time has indeed arrived for business to become far more open than it has been in the past, to anticipate calls for disclosure, to disclose without being asked its workings and its problems, to report its failures as well as its successes.

This policy was followed, not long ago, after a spate of stories appeared about American corporations overseas bribing foreign government officials. Many firms suffered public disgrace as a result of such disclosures. To combat that public disgrace, one analyst suggested that business should have been prepared to stand up and say:

> Of course we bribe—so does everyone else, and that's the way you do business overseas. We don't see that it is the American government's business, since we're not violating any American law. If you want to do business in Saudi Arabia, you do business with the King's relatives. If foreign governments don't like our bribing them, then why don't the foreign countries prosecute?

He objected especially to the fact that, although the actions might have been unethical, they were not illegal, and questioned the U.S. government's intervention:

> The government doesn't legislate morality for anyone else anymore, so why is it legislating morality for businessmen overseas? No one would dream of legislating sexual morality for American students in Paris, but they want to legislate business morality for businessmen in Paris.[7]

One Washington, D.C. public relations expert advises: "tell them before they ask—it's easier that way." [8] By spending more time with the media providing answers that are responsive to public concerns, business could well be on the way toward restoring favorable public confidence.

The answers, however, must come from the top. Frank Shakespeare, president of RKO General, says chief executives have "an enormous responsibility of leading in areas that go beyond running the internal mechanisms" of a corporation:

> Part of the leadership of a free society has to come from business. No junior in a corporation will step out an eighth of an inch beyond what his chief executive officer has said, becuse that's not prudent. So the chief executive not only sets the rules for himself, but he sets the parameters for the whole corporation—all of his juniors. And if he is afraid of a bad editorial in *The New York Times,* or a tough comment on the network, and if he keeps his head down, that whole corporation keeps its head down, and a voice is lost—a tough, argumentative voice to the American system.[9]

Marsha Ludwig, a reporter for *Forbes Magazine,* has borne out Shakespeare's thesis by finding a trend that younger executives are actually less willing than the older ones to say anything of substance for publication: "They are more likely to fill you with jargon or executive terminology, and say nothing. And, in fairness to the junior executive, he may well be afraid of being misquoted or cited in the story at all. There may be nothing but risk for him in talking to the press." [10] H. Stuart Harrison, chairman of Cleveland-Cliffs Iron Company, supports Frank Shakespeare: "Companies today must realize that getting their stories across is one of the jobs of chief executive officers. Otherwise, business as we know it is done for." [11]

In summary, public activism on the part of chief executives, according to management expert Peter Drucker, has proved considerably more effective than the traditional approaches to "public relations," by which a firm responded to inquiry. For one thing, only the chief executive has the ability and the authority to speak for a firm, or to commit a firm to a course of action.

To help cope with these new demands on a corporation executive's time, Drucker suggests American management should study the Japanese version of management, in which the top people do not manage the company (they leave that to managing directors). Rather, they manage "relations" with trade groups and associations, labor, the press, and government—and their relationship with government is an intimate one.[12]

CHAPTER 2

The Interview: How and Why

The most effective way to get a message across is to discuss the message directly with the audience for whom the message is intended. The next best method is to send a personal letter or memo describing the message. Both such approaches are used every day in business. Yet, when trying to convince large numbers of people of the validity of an argument, or when seeking to give news of an organization, such approaches become impractical as well as time-consuming and enormously costly. They may also be unsuccessful. The alternative is an exchange with the people who work in the mass media—the radio, television, and newspaper reporters who are interested, or who can become interested, in some aspect of a company's work.

Despite all of its real or perceived faults, the American news system has developed, over more than two centuries of relatively unfettered operation, into the most efficient vehicle in the world for communicating a message to the public. At no cost to the communicator, any message potentially can be presented to an audience of ten or 20 million people. However, success with the press, as success in any other endeavor, does not come easily.

Business, particularly large corporations that want to win back a share of the public trust and confidence, must start with the twin premises that public support is a derivative of public communication. Thus, it quickly becomes clear that one of the main duties of leaders of organizations is to communicate with the public through the news media.

The task of communicating with the press is less foreboding, of course, when management is doing its job properly. It is a maxim that bad news is more likely to receive coverage, for as one expert puts it: "The opportunity for getting on the front page is significantly enhanced by screwing up."

Yet, for some executives, the most harrowing moments of their careers are when they must face a reporter, a camera, and a microphone, or take a reporter's call. While the executive may have been briefed in advance by a public relations officer prior to meeting the reporter, once the contact is established, the manager is on his own with the reporter. When a reporter calls, it is virtually certain that a story will appear and that it will be written whether the source cooperates or not. More than likely, however, without the source's cooperation, the story will come out with wrong or inadequate facts, misleading implications or interpretations, or wrong conclusions. It thus behooves management to cooperate and communicate, although there is no legal obligation to do so.

One of the most frequent complaints of reporters when they are working on a story and making a legitimate attempt to gain access to an executive is that they are told he is not available for comment. At best, the reporter will then say that the company declines comment; at worst, the reporter only leaves the impression that something is being hidden and that whatever is being reported on has some merit. In addition, shunting reporters from the executive to the public relations office can infuriate them when they are working on a significant story. Reporter Sylvia Chase of ABC-TV's *20/20* newsmagazine says, "What you really want to do is to talk to the president of the company. Why? Because they are people who run corporations. Public relations people don't run corporations." [1]

Furthermore, reporters have a right to expect that key company executives will make themselves available in bad times as well as in good. This expectation is especially strong when an executive has cultivated the press during the good times; the manager who makes himself available only at his convenience does so at his own peril. Reporters feel used when an executive who previously took all their calls suddenly cannot be reached; they do not easily forget the rebuff.

As survivors, however, business managers instinctively recognize the dangers inherent in announcing unfavorable results. H. R. Caffyn's "Law of According To" suggests that "The rosier the news, the higher-ranking the official who announces it." [2]

MEETING THE PRESS: SIMPLE RULES

The most common form of communication with the news media is the interview, whether it be a telephone interview, a chat on the sidewalk, a sit-down interview in an office, or a live interview in a studio. By following a few simple rules, potentially disastrous situations can be turned into successful encounters. These rules involve preparing something substantive to say; knowing the reporter in order to anticipate his questions; and knowing what to do—and what not to do—after the interview.

PROVIDE SUBSTANCE

Before going into an interview, consider the points that need to be made, and have something substantive to say. Do not be afraid to help set the agenda, or to take the initiative when a reporter calls. Often the course or tone of a story can be influenced by introducing information or ideas the reporter may not have considered. This does not mean that you should change the subject when something unpleasant arises, but it does mean that after questions are answered, you can turn the reporter's attention back to the points you want to make.

When a company wants to get on the front page, the executive must say something specific that will interest the reporter. A manager might complain that there is never anything in the news about his company, yet the potential for making news is almost always present. For example, a public relations counsel has boasted that he can pick up the front page of nearly any major newspaper in the country and find a place for his client to get in the news. Whether it is inflation, government controls, corporate profits, taxes, international trade, defense spending or the energy crisis, most large companies deal with these topics one way or another every day in a way that affects the public. Thus, a manager may insert newsworthy comments if he plays up to a reporter's news instincts.

A live broadcast interview offers a unique opportunity to get across one's points. Tom Brokaw, host of the "Today" show, invited two spokeswomen for the National Women's Conference in Houston to appear live on the show. Before they went on the air, both women were briefed by a public relations counselor: "Remember, it's live television. You've got six minutes. Do you want to answer Tom's questions or do you want to get across what you came here to say?" Brokaw says that no matter what question he asked, they would go back to their prepared points.[3] Brokaw later told a business audience: "Now that's a very useful technique, and I wish you'd keep it in this room. I get into a problem as an interrogator or an interviewer. If I interrupt, I am accused of being rude by the audience. Or if I don't interrupt, I am accused by the people who are disagreeing. It's a no-win situation." Vice-President Mondale appeared on the show at about the same time, Brokaw said, "and he just ran roughshod over me. I finally broke in and said, 'Mr. Vice President?' He said, 'Excuse me a minute,' and he kept on talking. Well, what do you do? I finally ended the interview by saying, 'Here's the man who ended the filibuster in Washington but has learned something in the process.' It's a tough business."

ANTICIPATE

"Anticipate" is perhaps the most important word to remember in preparing for any public encounter. Consider what the audience wants to hear, what they want to find out. There is considerable merit in practicing or rehearsing for an interview.

Indeed, former President Ford, in preparing for a news conference during which he might be called upon to discuss nearly any subject of public importance, would routinely spend four or five hours being grilled by his staff the day before he faced the reporters. Far from being a waste of a president's time, such sessions prepared him to answer questions intelligently in front of millions of people and served the dual purpose of keeping him informed on a variety of public issues.

While most managers in business would find spending the same amount of time as President Ford spent in preparation an inordinate period of time to spend preparing for interviews in their more narrowly defined areas of responsibility, it would be wise for them to set aside an hour or so several days prior to an interview to prepare. Along with several colleagues or subordinates, write out the most hostile questions that you could conceivably be asked. Imagine for a moment that the reporter has the same knowledge of your business and the same basic facts that you have (although nine times out of ten he will not). How sharply could the questions be asked? What are the best answers? The questions you or your staff come up with probably will be more vicious than those from any reporter, and answers should be prepared for each question. Failure to do so is a serious mistake, for in dealing with the press, one rule applies: "There is no such thing as a pleasant surprise." [4] It is always helpful to determine the scope of an interview at the time it is set up. Although no good reporter will consent to submitting questions in advance, it is not improper to inquire about the general areas of inquiry. Your preparation will be tailored differently if the topic is the recall of faulty parts, the recent resignation of a senior executive, or the suit by a consumer group.

In most cases, however, the subject will be fairly obvious. Reporters tend to adhere to topical news stories, so that if corporate bribery is the current hot topic and if your company has been implicated, a call from a reporter should signify an interview in which corporate bribery will be raised. Moreover, there is nothing monolothic about the news media's approach to any story, so that business can to a considerable extent pick its target media and tailor its approach to that outlet's needs. In that respect, it is useful to try to determine how and when the story will be used. A 30-second add-on to the evening news roundup will dictate a different approach than a Sunday profile of a company's product or service, or a trend story on an industry. Furthermore, a business executive's interview with a news magazine, a local radio station, a network television crew, a wire service reporter, or a suburban weekly paper may result in five vastly different stories. Unless he understands that different media have different needs, the executive may wonder whether all five reporters were present in the same room at the same time.

KNOW THE REPORTER

Another essential requisite for a successful interview is getting to know the reporter. Why type of stories does he normally cover? If he is an investigative reporter or a columnist, does he have a known bias about business? Is he educated in the language and interests of business, or will he need help interpreting jargon? Has he written about your industry before? It is useful to maintain a reference file on individual reporters but if no such file exists, try to establish some common ground with the reporter by discussing sports, weather, travel, or some other common, noncontroversial subject at the outset. It will pay off as the reporter beings to see you as a person instead of an institution, and both of you will feel more relaxed during the business part of your discussion.

Recently a political scientist called a top political reporter in Washington and asked him how he decided which of the many presidential primary campaigns to cover. The reporter answered, half-jokingly, "Arbitrarily." The vignette, with a kernel of truth, illustrates the freedom the press often has in deciding whether to cover a story.

In making these decisions, reporters and editors will go first and most often to sources of news that can give them what they are looking for: a colorful quote, an inside tip, a complete hard news story, or, sometimes, someone whose company they enjoy. A business manager also should make every effort to get to know and enjoy reporters because that is one important way of ensuring follow-up coverage and favorable treatment. Think back to your last encounter with a reporter: Was it pleasant, or merely civil? If you were the reporter, would you want to see and be with that executive again?

There are dangers, however, in becoming too friendly with reporters.

Thus, Les Whitten, the investigative reporter associated with Jack Anderson, who admits to a sense of outrage against big business, has given an example:

You don't have to talk to me. But you have your rights. If I wrong you, you can sue hell out of me. You are not obliged when the hangman comes to put the noose around your own neck. And yet, time and time again, we somehow get past the PR person who's been hired to keep us away from the chief executive. We get the chief executive—he's a nice guy, smoking a pipe, and he says, "Gee, he's just a reporter. You know, these reporter boys are nice fellows. Why don't I level with him?"

The next thing you know, the company executive has hanged himself, the PR person has shot himself, and the executive vice president is rubbing his hands because he knows he's going to get the president's job. And all this need never have happened: you don't have any obligation to talk to me when I call you up.

Let me give an example of how we got a man to hang himself. The story is about Senator George Murphy of California. Somebody had come in with a wild tip that Murphy had been getting some money out of a company. It was late in the day and Jack Anderson said, "Well, I'll just take a chance and see if Murphy will hang himself." So he called up George Murphy and he said, "George, I have got proof that is going to make your hair stand on end, but because you're a special friend of mine"—he was no more Jack's friend than he was the wind—"I'm going to give you a chance to respond to this before I go into print with it. I understand you've been getting a large sum of money from this company. . . ."

Well, by the time Jack had finished talking, Senator Murphy thought that Jack had proof that he had about $200,000 a year coming in, so he said, "Jack, nothing like that ever happened. I swear it never happened." And Jack said, "Senator, I'm going to hate to make a liar out of you in print this way, but I'm going to have to do it. I'll give you 45 minutes to re-think this before I sit down at the typewriter."

About 45 minutes later George Murphy comes over and he says, I swear to God, Jack, it was only $15,000 a year. . . .

Half the time when I call I simply don't have the facts and I'm trying to con you out of them. I'm calling up and saying, "Well, didn't such-and-such happen?" I may have nothing whatever to back that up except an intuition, and I put that question to you.

Your answer should be, "Well, what do you have that would indicate that's true? You should try to find out what I know. Instead,
you answer my most fishing question, and just put the hook right
smack in your mouth, and I'm glad to jerk you out of the water, and
out you come, panting on the beach the next day in Jack Anderson's
column or TV show.

I've done this hundreds and hundreds of times, and I've found
when I can get to your chief executive, invariably I can get a heck of
a lot more out of him than I can get out of his PR person.[5]

Not all investigative reporters are as clever as Whitten. If his state of
mind and his approach can be understood, or at least anticipated, the
seemingly hostile, probing questions from other reporters will be easier
to deal with.

GETTING QUOTED

Some people who seem to have a knack for making news skillfully
prepare for an interview or a public appearance by thinking up a single
sentence, or a catchy phrase, that summarizes their views on an issue.
The media almost universally love such quick summaries, will look for
them, and, if they are good, will use them. Of course, the reverse is also
true: A long rambling, disjointed response, with awkward pauses between awkward clauses, will practically ensure that no part of the interview will be used (sometimes that may be a desirable objective). The
dean of a leading eastern school spent two and a half hours talking with
a reporter who was doing a major story on a topic in which the dean was
a recognized authority. But, the reporter did not use a word of what the
dean said and did not cite him as a source. His problem was that the
dean's esoteric, reflective, and convoluted sentences disguised the information contained in his answers and would have been deadly dull in
print or on the air.

By way of contrast, when Ralph Nader testified against the major oil
companies, he was asked why he thought solar energy was not being
developed. He replied, "Because ARCO doesn't own the sun." Although
it came across that way, that was not a spontaneous response. It was
carefully considered in advance, probably rehearsed, and it was the
quote that the media used when they wrote the synopsis of the day's
testimony. In like manner, when actress Jane Fonda appeared before a
large antinuclear rally in Washington after the Three Mile Island incident, she boisterously delivered from her address one sentence which

summarized what the crowd thought the whole rally was all about. Calling for the resignation of the Secretary of Energy because of his pronuclear bias, she shouted, "Putting James Schlesinger in charge of nuclear energy is like putting Dracula in charge of a blood bank." That was the quotation the media all used. It made her point, and it was brief.

THE FOLLOW-UP

For a variety of reasons, not every story will be favorable, and not every story will appear as the source wishes. Despite the best efforts of a business manager, there will be times when a quotation will be rearranged, facts omitted, or when no story will appear at all. It is tempting, as a professional to whom perfection might seem an ideal, to straighten out any misconceptions or bad wording, but managers need to be aware of the pitfalls in following up on a story.

No matter what happens, the reporter will always have the last word. It will be apparent when the interview is over whether it has gone well, whether the reporter is dealing in good faith, or whether he has an antibusiness bias.

"Never argue with a man who buys ink by the barrel," suggests William Greener, a former Ford Administration spokesman.[6] His rule merits consideration and should be followed—unless it seems that the reporter has made something other than an honest mistake. If there are solid reasons for believing that the reporter is carrying out a vendetta, there may be grounds for a letter to the editor, a request for air time on a station to clarify the impressions left, another interview, or, in flagrant abuses, a lawsuit.

News that is improperly reported, or inadequately treated, contributes in almost every case, to the impression that the press may be hostile. An executive who gives an interview will be much closer to the facts and nuances of every word than the general reader or listener. There is always a tendency to think ill of an article or report that does not read exactly the way you would have written it, contains one or two negative comments, or gets a few facts garbled.

Reporters, it should be remembered, are frequently on a deadline when they call, and want to have an answer in fifteen minutes. Business managers would obviously prefer to consider things carefully, and prepare, and clear statements before they put them out. But if a story is written and its perspective seems slightly askew, it would be better to work toward building a longer term relationship in which the reporter might be educated in your perspective rather than calling the reporter's editor and complaining.

The important thing to remember is that the reader is influenced by the overall tone or theme of a story—and seldom by an individual detail. To understand how an article will impress an outside observer, it must be read objectively, as though by someone not in possession of any of the facts.

Another element to consider in following up on a story is that once a statement has been uttered, it is irretrievable. Stories abound of public relations people who have been fired because they were unable to suppress truthful comments or statements made by management during on-the-record interviews. Another story, told by Professor Louis Banks of MIT, concerns the "egomanical executive":

"A president of a middle-sized New England firm thought he was worthy of an interview in a metropolitan daily. Wondrously, his PR man was able to bring it off—only to be fired the day after the story appeared because the interviewer had described the executive as 'swarthy.'"[7] Public relations people have no more control over an interview than do the executives being interviewed, and they almost never see an article before it appears in print.

CHAPTER 3

The Media

ELECTRONIC MEDIA

TELEVISION

In the span of a single generation, television has become the most pervasive and profitable media source of entertainment, information, and influence in American society. The growth and development of the television industry has been phenomenal; it is the fastest-growing medium in history, having gained a far greater dominance over thoughts and suggestions than any society has yet witnessed. In 1950, there were 98 stations on the air. By the end of the decade of the 1970s, there were 727 commercial stations and an additional 259 educational stations operating within the United States.[1]

Ninety-eight percent of the households in America own a television set, and 46 percent own two or more sets—for a total of more than 135 million TV sets in use in the United States. The average American family's television is in use for an incredible six hours a day. It should come as no surprise that a recent poll by the Roper organization revealed that 65 percent of all Americans get all of their news from television and radio broadcasts. As a further illustration of telelvision's influence, Charles Ferris, chairman of the Federal Communications Commission, has estimated that when the average student graduates from high school, he has spent 12,000 hours in the classroom, and 25,000 hours before a television.[2]

Bolstering Ferris' estimate is another poll, conducted over a two-year period, which revealed that 44 percent of the four-to-six-year-old children surveyed preferred watching television to "being with Daddy." [3]

And since so many of the entertainment programs on television shows reflect, as one critic called it, "the liberal antibusiness bias of a group of

22

200 script writers and producers in Hollywood," it should become clear that business cannot leave alone to television the way the business world is perceived by the public at large.[4]

And while much discussion is heard on television news broadcasts about "monopolies," particularly in the energy industry, the three major networks control 95 percent of the national shows. (The top four oil companies control only 35 percent of the petroleum market.)

All of this information should make it clear to the American business community that it behooves them to have their story told with greater accuracy and completeness on television. To achieve this objective, they must first understand how television and radio stations seek, prepare, edit, and share their news package.

While media profits are seldom discussed in the same context as profits of the energy, steel, or automobile industries, television is almost four times more profitable than the average American industry. Commercial television stations and networks had an average pretax profit of 20 percent in the most recent years for which figures are available, higher than almost any other industry.[5] It is ironic, then, that this medium has been kept alive and has been nurtured by the very business system which, business managers claim, has misrepresented them so seriously in news and entertainment programs. In a recent year the business community spent $8 billion on television advertising—at about $61,500 per prime-time minute.

Despite this, a survey by *TV Guide* over a three-month period showed that 95 percent of all economic and business news on network television was negative news, or was portrayed to the audience as negative news. By contrast, a survey by the Yankelovich organization shows that fewer than 15 percent of the public believes newspaper coverage of business is unfair.[6]

Social critics charge that television has fundamentally altered the way society perceives itself, and the way it receives news. This has come about in a relatively short period, and its impact has yet to be fully measured. Certainly television has promoted a certain amount of homogeneity in American society. However, the passive acceptance of television, whatever its psychological or social impact—will long be debated. As Lance Morrow contended in a *Time* essay:

> . . . television's greatest consequence has been to impart sheer velocity to ideas and fads. From antiwar protests to disco dancing, such trends tend to start on the coasts and then get transfused with

astonishing speed into the life of the heartland between. TV thus serves to obliterate regional and local distinctions, to create national social values.[7]

Yet, network television news has expanded in scope and in length in the last half-generation, and the length of a network news show may double again within the next few years. Until 1963, at 7 o'clock the standard local TV station carried 15 minutes of locally originated news and five minutes of weather and sports, followed by 15 minutes of network news. At 11 o'clock there was ten minutes and news and five minutes of weather and sports. Today, in most cities, the local station runs 60 or 90 minutes of locally originated news followed by a half hour of network news. Thus, there is a two-hour segment of news every night, back-to-back, and at 11 o'clock, another half hour. The impact of this expansion has become all the more dramatic with live mini-cams, color, and satellite transmissions from all over the world, and all the money, background, and theatrical technique that go with it.

THE NETWORKS

Most of the commercial television stations—about 84 percent of them—are affiliated with one of the major networks, CBS, NBC, or ABC. Each of these affiliated stations receives from the network with which it is associated a significant portion of its entertainment programming, as well as the national evening news programs, around which each builds its own local coverage. The influence of the networks' news broadcasts has expanded greatly since 1963, when both CBS and NBC expanded their nightly news from 15 minutes to 30; ABC followed in 1967. The networks began running more national news and expanding news analysis of some of the local stories they covered. And they received an increasing portion of the national audience, until today the three networks' early evening news shows have a combined audience of 50 million people. CBS' Walter Cronkite has insisted that 30 minutes is not enough time to cover the day's events and has long advocated expanding network news to a full hour. The inadequacy of even this treatment of news has given rise to additional public affairs and news programing, such as NBC's "Special Segment" each evening; Public Broadcasting's two shows, "MacNeil/Lehrer Report" and "Agronsky & Company"; CBS' "Sixty Minutes" (which climbed to the top of the Nielsen ratings in 1979); ABC's "20/20," and the Sunday shows: "Face The Nation," "Meet The Press," and "Issues and Answers."

Network news is assembled in New York and Washington through a rigorous debating, editing, and selection process. The nature of television news dictates that a majority of the stories must have action film or visual stimulation, which, of course, somewhat limits the type of stories than can be covered. The advent of the portable mini-cam and electronic taping equipment has given news more immediate punch and has cost the networks millions of dollars. These innovations, however, have not necessarily made coverage more analytical or impartial.

The networks maintain camera crews and correspondents in the major cities: New York, Washington, Atlanta, Chicago, Los Angeles, some on the road, and major overseas capitals. They also accept film "feeds" from their affiliates—local stations around the country who purchase programing from the networks and share their own significant news stories. Usually, about 15 to 18 stories can be squeezed into a 30-minute broadcast after allowing time for advertisements and opening and closing the program. That leaves about one-and-a-half or two minutes allotted for each story, and the majority of these must have film (even, it seems, if the film shows a foreign correspondent merely standing in front of a famous building with a microphone in hand). It does not leave much time for in-depth coverage, but rather results in what Cronkite has called the "attention-arresting" lead sentence and the "hyper-compression" of news, which negate accuracy and balance. Television provides, at best, only a headline service.

Macroeconomics is often a major news story, and a reporter's job is made easier by the government and major trade groups which compile and hand out cumulative statistics in Washington and New York. As a result, business reporting on the typical network news program invariably includes closing averages on the major exchanges—with no explanation as to what the figures mean to the average viewer. The program may also include additional business-related news—perhaps the report of a price increase of a major industry such as automobiles, steel, or the change in leadership in a major firm. Missing is the art of microeconomic reporting by which the public might come to understand how a firm or a particular industry performs.

But since a good story must have good visuals to get on the air, television *news* is still television *entertainment*. That one requirement alone makes television's present format ill-equipped to deal with business and economic news, which normally is abstract, complex, and hard to visualize. Much of what businessmen say is complex, and television simply cannot or will not attempt to cope with complexity. Television is, as one critic has summarized, "impressions made, not arguments weighed." [8]

Sometimes, especially on local television news programs, assignment editors set out to make a point and dispatch reporters to collect information in support of a contention. This occasionally becomes painfully obvious, as occured when a New York City station, looking specifically for an economics professor—any economics professor—to denounce a Con Edison rate increase called a major university only to find that not a single professor in good conscience could make such a statement. The station went elsewhere looking for someone to present the opinions it wanted. This approach is a favorite reportorial tactic: finding a source with beliefs the reporter has previously decided are needed.

In another instance, during a brief strike by state police, a local television newsman in New York randomly interviewed Connecticut motorists on the Merritt Parkway, asking whether they would exceed the 55 mile-per-hour speed limit despite the fact that police would not be patrolling. Not a single respondent said he/she would exceed the limit; they cited a variety of reasons: fuel economy at lower speeds, respect for the law, more safety at 55, and so on. Yet in his closing comment on the broadcast, the newsman—as if expecting New York-bound motorists to speed in spite of evidence to the contrary—warned viewers to slow down coming into New York.

The rule of thumb for the opening of a broadcast is to get action into the first 30 seconds of a program, or viewers will switch to the competition. If enough viewers switch, ratings go down, stations cannot charge as much for advertising, and they lose money. As a result, television's requirement for visual impact results in distortion of perspective. Therefore, the disproportionate number of fires, bombings, auto accidents, demonstrations, and pickets presented on television might be deemed unrepresentative of the day's events. Too often, what appears on the screen is an isolated moment of symbolic action.

When President Carter welcomed China's Vice Premier Deng Xiao-Ping to the United States in a ceremony on the South Lawn of the White House, it was an historic moment: the symbolic first steps of two great nations joining together in friendship. Both leaders made brief remarks and exchanged greetings. What did the networks show? They showed two reporters from a socialist newspaper being removed from the press area for heckling. Watching the evening news, one might think it was a major disaster in the embryonic relationship between superpowers. Yet, the next day, in the national newspapers of record, *The New York Times* and *The Washington Post*, the heckling was hardly mentioned. It paled in significance next to the symbolism of the event and the words of the two heads of state.

Television's thirst for visuals can work against would-be newsmakers, or it can work for them, depending on how it is approached. That is why electioneering candidates ride in antique car parades, or on floats, or march down the avenue (behind the press truck), and perform all sorts of similar stunts. By competing with their opponents for attention, the public performances of candidates are reduced to television shows, and they can reach millions more people than the meager crowd in front of them.

Unfortunately, most business people have been slow or reluctant to develop the instinct for the camera angle and the newsmaking stunt that their counterparts in politics and sports have acquired. Nor are they inclined to seek more media experience if they are once burned.

It is difficult, for instance, to imagine a broadcast station reporting on business executives in the way they report the activities of sports figures or politicians. Everything about the sports' and political leaders' lives is disclosed: salaries, benefits packages, trades, job changes, physical stamina, new strategies, and assessments of the competition. But the broadcast media tell us very little about the executives of major companies in our communities.

Some of those in broadcasting agree, and they sharpen the self-criticism. Westinghouse radio newsman Bill Scott has remarked,

> There is virtually no one in broadcasting who does a very good job of reporting business or economic news. Very few [reporters] put it in terms that are meaningful and understandable to most people.
>
> We hear a lot about cost of living indices, we hear a great deal about the International Monetary Fund, we hear about M1 and M2—but I'm not sure anybody translates that into what it means to the farmer in Iowa, the woman in Manhattan, the man in the Bronx.[9]

And the notion that television coverage has become oversimplified and unsophisticated has been acknowledged by some renowned performers and practioners. "I can't defend how television has covered the economy and business developments," says "Today" host Tom Brokaw.

> I think that we have done less than an adequate job. This is a mass audience you're dealing with—not people with a highly developed sense of what's going on in the economy . . . people to whom M1 is maybe a rifle. They have no sense of what the money supply is, don't know what the Federal Reserve is.
>
> I do think that we have a better sense of where we're going with it, and if there is anything going on within my business, there is a

kind of crash course in the development of people who understand the economy and understand business developments.[10]

Bob Flaherty of *Forbes* magazine believes the problem of TV and business reporting goes far deeper than the deficiencies of the news departments:

> I think the media in general obviously create an anti-business bias, but there is little that anyone can do about it. TV does the job when viewers are children. If you look at almost any of the TV series, the businessman is projected as lecherous, greedy, immoral, cowardly, so narrow-minded he cannot see any social goal beyond making money, mixed up with organized crime, a corrupter of government at home and abroad. I don't think this portrayal is done because there is any anti-business bias; it's just that villains make stories exciting, and it's a profitable activity.[11]

Robert Bleiberg of *Barron's*, charges, "Television, notably the network news programs and documentaries, goes out of its way to exaggerate the flaws of business and minimize the achievements."[12] William Small, a vice president and former Washington bureau chief of CBS, says business people would like to sanitize their statements through public relations people: "Take the case of Red Dye No. 2. We went to the company for an interview. They wouldn't give an interview but would give a 90-second statement if we promised not to edit one word of it. The whole function of journalism relates to proper editing of raw material. You don't just turn over a glob of time to an advocate and say, 'That's yours.'"[13]

LOCAL TELEVISION STATIONS

The TV news with which most businesses will have to deal will originate at stations in their own communities. The process by which a local station presents the news may be divided into three areas: the newsroom, the control room, and the set. In the newsroom there is an assignment editor working with the news editor to decide where to send the camera crews and reporters on any day to gather local stories. Both types of editor, as well as the news correspondent, are excellent people to get to know, since stories on local stations originate from several sources. One source is the editors or reporters, who might think that an event in town, such as a convention, or a visiting dignitary, ought to receive some attention. Other sources include stories in a newspaper that have possibilities for adaptation to TV; wire service stories; or, less frequently, a tip from an outside source, such as a press release or phone call. But the decisions are made by the assignment and news editors, and the overriding consideration must be that the story affords the possibility of visual action.

In the newsroom, correspondents may be typing their stories, preparing to read them on camera, or feeding stories to the anchor person to read. The newsroom also houses wire service machines ticking away and teletyping the news from around the world.

During the broadcast, the program director sits inside the control booth monitoring a battery of television screens mounted along one wall. Each screen carries a different image, including the competition's channels, the transmission of the station itself, the network feed, shots from the various floor cameras in the studio, the next scheduled advertisements, and perhaps the station logo.

The studio, or news set, is where the correspondents sit when they are on camera. It is usually a room about the size of a basketball court, with concrete walls and large drapes to absorb excess sound. The room is chilled by air conditioning, but the set is hot under the brilliant lights. Two or three large cameras on wheeled tripods are pushed around the room by cameramen according to instructions received on headphones from the program director. The angle of the cameras is constantly being changed, since television is considered boring or unimaginative if any one shot is held more than seven seconds. This makes for constant action on the screen. The news announcer may read the news from a script before him or from a TelePrompTer mounted on the camera. As the program is about to begin, all is quiet in the studio, the director's voice comes over the loudspeaker with a countdown, the red light comes on and the performance begins.

Sometimes, in reporting, television finds that its own technological sophistication gets in the way of common sense. Not long ago a gunman walked into a building in a major city, seized several hostages, and then made himself available to the news media—while the siege was still underway. Local television and radio took the man up on his offer and provided him with *live* coverage.

A few days later, news director Virgil Dominic of Station WJKW in Ohio admitted the new depths to which television journalism had sunk: "We are glorifying lawbreakers," he wrote.

> We are making heros out of nonheros. In effect, we are losing control over our news departments; we are being used. . . . Extensive coverage by television only serves to encourage imitators or dis-

turbed people in general, and will contribute to endangering the lives of innocent people. . . . Despite the tremendous competition that exists among local television news teams, we will no longer automatically grant live coverage to future Cory Moores. In fact, we will not only limit our coverage of such men and the incidents they create, we might not cover them at all. We are going to do this even if it means that we lose part of our audience. This does not mean that we are going to ignore news events, but rather that we are going to report them in reasonable perspective. . . . If we do not take the first step to regain control of our newsrooms, then the matter will get entirely out of hand.[14]

One technique used occasionally in television interviews is called "confrontation journalism." Just when the interview subject . . . begins to act complacently, the reporter confronts him with a damning document, or quotation, to contradict him, and generally the composure of the person being interviewed instantly dissolves.

The confrontation technique is so heavily weighted in favor of the journalist as to be intrinsically unfair. Bill Brown, a former "60 Minutes" producer, says,

On one side you have professionals, people accustomed to dealing with cameras and the rest of the technical side of it; on the other side is someone who might never have been close to a TV camera before. Then they get a tight shot of his face, and of course he doesn't look comfortable. He doesn't know about eye contact with the camera, so his eyes are shifting. And all the while Mike Wallace is talking to him—and Mike is a very imposing character.[15]

Cutaways

Often, television reporters in an interview situation appear to care as much about their questions as the subject's answers. When an interview is over, for instance, the cameras are turned around to film the reporter asking the questions again, this time in a much more polished and precise manner, looking directly into the eyes of the interview subject. They may also prepare film of the reporter knowingly studying the subject, nodding, frowning, or lifting an eyebrow.

Former CBS reporter Daniel Schorr was interviewed for "60 Minutes." The taped interview lasted an hour and 15 minutes; the transcript runs 75 pages. The first question that appeared on the air comes up on page 21 of the transcript; the first 20 pages had been consumed with reporter Mike Wallace heaping praise on Schorr, and softening him up for tough questions.[16]

The only real way to maintain control over a television interview is to accede to a live interview or to a taped one where only a limited period of time, such as three minutes or less is allowed. Otherwise, much of what you say may be edited out, important points may be lost, and your words may not be presented fairly.

RADIO

As Roper's polling has shown, 65 percent of all Americans receive almost all of their news from radio and television. And if television is an all-pervasive and inadequate medium for telling business' story, radio is even more pervasive.

There are more than 425 million radios in use today throughout the United States—about two radios for every man, woman, and child. That fact is all the more remarkable when one considers that the first radio station took to the air in 1927 (KDKA, in Pittsburgh). Within two years after that, there were 600 stations on the air, and, within 20 years, there were more than a thousand. By the time radio celebrated its fiftieth year, in 1977, there were more than 8000 stations on the air.[17]

Radio advertising draws in about 7 percent of the total number of advertising dollars spent in the United States, about $2.2 billion in a recent year. By contrast, television attracts about triple that amount, and newspapers four times that amount.[18]

There are more than 4500 AM stations and 3700 FM stations. A majority of the AM stations, about 62 percent, are affiliated with a major broadcasting network, NBC, CBS, ABC, or Mutual Broadcasting. In addition, others are affiliated with a number of smaller, regional networks, such as Westinghouse Broadcasting, the Tobacco Network in the south, and so on.

Networks provide stations with news, commentary, and sometimes entertainment. In the case of the major networks, such programing usually originates in New York or Los Angeles and is transmitted over leased telephone lines, Most radio stations rely almost exclusively for their news upon the wire services. AP, UPI, and Dow Jones all offer a "radio wire" written in shorter, sportier phrases. These stories come across to the radio news desk in far less detail than the wire or print stories from which they are drawn. The radio news package provides only news updates on significant stories in the headlines without the supporting details or explanations. The importance of these headline-service packages on the wires cannot be underestimated, however. For instance, the AP broadcast wire serves more than 5000 subscriber members. And AP in the mid-1970s added a voice network to its services.

Radio News Sources

Radio stations acquire news of local interest from the print media in their area, albeit sometimes in a roundabout manner. For instance, when a newspaper in a big city breaks a story, it will share carbon copies of the reporter's story with the local bureau of the wire service to which it subscribes. The wire service then rewrites it in abbreviated form and sends it out on the wire to other subscribers, including broadcast members, who may put it on the air at once. Thus, news in the morning paper, which is printed near midnight, will be on the radio news broadcasts before the morning rush hour begins.

Voices of News

Radio broadcasters, because of the peculiar nature of their medium, seek voices other than the announcer's for variety of presentation. For that reason, stations in bigger markets might employ "experts" or "contributing reporters" such as representatives from brokerage houses; in addition, the voices of foreign correspondents are sometimes used (as if to prove they are really on location) despite the poor audio quality, which may make the reporter sound as though he is under water or on a roller coaster.

All-news Radio

One recent innovation in radio broadcasting is the all-news format; the first all-news station, WINS in New York City, went on the air in 1965. Within three years there were 25 all-news stations in major cities. Thus, in some markets, there are stations capable of delivering 168 live hours of news a week.

PRINT MEDIA

NEWSPAPERS

The American newspaper system as we have known it is fading away—consumed by broadcast competition. While there is an elite minority in the country who seriously seek more details about the news, or prefer a more rational, analytical view of the world than they get in broadcasts, this minority constitutes a shrinking percentage of news consumers.

Since the heyday of the big-city newspaper in the twenties, newspaper competition within major cities has been dying out. In 1923, 502 American cities had two or more daily newspapers—about 38.7 percent of the cities. Fifty years later, only 37 cities could boast two or more papers—only 2.4 percent of all American cities.[19]

The actual number of American dailies has remained surprisingly constant in light of these percentages, at around 1760 newspapers, since World War II, but most of the growth in the number of newspapers, has been in suburban areas. However, there is a vast difference between the contents of a suburban paper and a central city newspaper, which emphasizes national and international news, may exert considerable power, and generate excitement.

As an illustration of the decline of newspapers, consider three major cities: Washington, New York, and Los Angeles. Fifteen years ago there were seven newspapers in New York, the largest, most important, most influential market in the United States, both for money and ideas. There were the *Daily Mirror* and *The New York News, The New York Times* and *The New York-Herald Tribune*, two of the largest circulation papers in the country. In the afternoon there were *The New York Journal-American* (the New York flag of Hearst), the *New York Telegram and Sun* (the flag of Scripps-Howard), and *The Post*. In that fifteen-year period, four of those seven New York newspapers have died: the *Daily Mirror*, which was the second largest circulation in the country; *The Herald-Tribune*, the second most prestigious paper in the United States at one time; *The Journal-American*, and *The World Telegram and Sun*.

In Washington in 1969, there were three newspapers: *The Post* in the morning, *The Star* and *The News* in the afternoon. The *News* has died. Washington is left with two newspapers, and the *Star* is being kept from going under by Time-Life, which owns it. In Los Angeles, 15 years ago, there were two newspapers in the morning and two in the afternoon; now there is one in the morning and one in the afternoon.[20]

What all this means is that the public is being treated to only one set of views. A second opinion, which is vital to balanced discourse and exchange, has been eliminated in most major cities.

Since most of the public must now rely upon broadcast news, this may effect deep psychological, political and societal changes. As Frank Shakespeare pointed out in his remarks at New York University in 1978: "If the way you perceive news through print is different than the way you perceive it through radio and television, then something fundamental will happen to your society." [21] It seems obvious that the perception will always be different. Three personality factors intrude upon the reception of news reported by various media: the way words are strung together, the tones of voice or inflections of speech, the general appearance of the newscaster and the facial expressions with which he punctuates the news. Newspapers offer one of these intrusions: the way the words are strung together. Radio offers two: the word structure and the inflections of speech. Television suffers all three of these naturally imposed prejudicial elements. "But that is only the beginning of TV's natural handicaps. The newspapers need only the attention of the eyes. Radio needs only the ears. Television needs the attention of both eyes and ears." [22]

During the time that these subtleties were being examined and when major changes were afoot in the newspaper industry, the press began to turn the same kind of scrutiny on business and major companies that it had trained for years on government. Since then, it has become clear that business reporting is coming into its own as a strong and distinct discipline. As a result, the years ahead will be a period of revelation, probing, and—with some luck—better public understanding of how American business functions.

TRENDS IN REPORTING BUSINESS AND FINANCIAL NEWS

Reporting business and financial news has come a long way in recent years. While there is, today, greater recognition by the press of the impact of business reporting, business news has a long way to go before it achieves the same level of sophistication as political or sports reporting, whether on television, radio, or in print.

Bob Flaherty of *Forbes* magazine, who both practices and, as a hobby studies business journalism, recalls that 50 years ago, business journalism was an appendage of business and promotion. "It was the whore's nest of journalism," Flaherty says, "a number of business journalists were in the pay of the companies that they wrote about." [23] Of course, it was not all corruption. Part of the reason that business reporting was underplayed is that it was seen by reporters as boring, or, at best, less glamorous than other assignments.

"I recall that back in 1951, two of my friends, then young and now fairly distinguished, went to work for *Time* Magazine," reports Irving Kristol.

This was their first really professional job as writers. I went up to visit them and there they were, sharing one office and doing the business section of *Time*—they knew absolutely nothing about this.

The business section of *Time* was where you started young and untrained reporters. You didn't dare start them in the Sports Section, because they might make a mistake and that would be serious. You'd get a million letters. But business didn't matter—you just put them in the business section for a year or so, and then they all expected to get out and get into really serious journalism.

Kristol admits that *Time* has changed with time, and contends that the magazine's business reporting is now better by "a multiple of fifty." [24]

Ben Bradlee, executive editor of *The Washington Post,* discusses his early days at the paper:

Business wasn't legitimate news 25 years ago, when it operated in a comparative vacuum. Certainly the government wasn't looking over your shoulders then as now. *The Washington Post,* when I got there 14 years ago, had *two* people in its business and financial department. It's got 18 now, and that's rather small compared to *The New York Times.*[25]

If in previous generations it was considered boring to draw the assignment of covering business, times have changed. An old joke was that the reporter caught reading *The Wall Street Journal* in the newsroom would become the next financial editor. Today a reporter reading that same newspaper is likely to be checking on the progress of the stock in his or her portfolio.

If the question is: "How do today's newspapers cover business?" states David Laventhol, publisher of the Long Island newspaper *Newsday,* "then I think the answer is 'probably badly.' This is the most primeval area as far as the kind of coverage that newspapers give . . . all over the country. Part of the reason is that it traditionally has been a stepchild." [26]

Laventhol suggests that another reason may be that, when a business does not like what is written about it in the newspaper, it has the ability to sue more readily than the average person.

I think that has tended to discourage newspapers, particularly those that are sensitive to economic pressures, from going too deeply into business stories. But I think the main thing is, really, businesses have not been willing to let themselves be communicated with by journalists in the same fashion that other areas or subjects that are written about have. For example, when covering a story, a reporter likes to talk to the source or the subject of a story, and frequently when dealing with a business, they'll end up talking to the public affairs or public relations person, and that's discouraging.

Also, businesses do not like to give out any kind of information about their blemishes, and nobody's perfect, and I think that in terms of credibility in relationships with reporters, it probably helps to acknowledge some things that may not reflect absolutely favorably on business.

Bob Flaherty suggests that the conventional business press treats business much more gently and with less depth than the political press treats politicians, or the sports press treats baseball managers.

It's kind of upsetting to see how many company presidents claim that the business media is anti-business. Often the president of a company will have so little internal criticism that he's not really told the facts of life or what to expect from outside coverage. Our system was set up with the press as an adversary, so stories should be objective.[27]

To explain the business media's treatment of business, Flaherty explains:

The goal we have at *Forbes* is to say, "This is a good company BUT. . . . a bad company BUT. The "but" should always be there." I've often found that management mistakes favorable stories for unfavorable ones. I frequently tell them that I'll do a second story and then show them the difference.

Often a president will get upset over a single adjective. They'll misread a cliche and take it literally. Frequently a PR person will talk with you and laugh about the reaction that the top brass had in this, but there's very few that will have the guts to actually tell this reaction to the boss's face.

David Rubin, a journalism professor who has researched relations between business and the media, cites the statement by a Florida newspaper that the "business beat" of a newspaper is almost never clearly defined:

The business page in small-city dailies tends to become sort of a Sargasso Sea into which drifts all of the news debris that cannot otherwise be classified: real estate, construction, home-building, deed, mortgages, bankruptcies, new legal or medical practices being set up, scholarships being offered by business firms, fund drives led by business leaders, the mobile TB unit schedule, shopping center promotions, and sales—you name it.[28]

The typical daily newspaper's business page consists of stock reports, perhaps a few condensed handouts from the local businesses, maybe a wire service story from AP, UPI, or *The New York Times* Service. On the whole, the business pages of the average daily have been dismal and boring. There is usually little evidence that creative, enterprising reporting has taken place. Frequently, the business desk is understaffed, and the task of covering the business community with anything resembling enthusiasm or verve, may be perceived as insurmountable.

Some of the major metropolitan papers have made improvements, however. News of business is now appearing in many parts of the newspaper, including the front page, which should increase reader sophistication, and reporters from other beats are frequently responsible for the stories. The business and finance section of *Newsweek* has increased nearly 25 percent in size in the past 20 years, while only half as many stories are presented, indicating that each contains greater detail and less information drawn from public relations handouts. *Business Week* employs a writer who covers the progress and effectiveness of environmental legislation, the economic impact of environmental cleanup, and the success or failure of individual companies in this area. The magazine has also made corporate responsibility a separate beat for another staffer. *The Wall Street Journal* has the "absolutely accurate eye for the importance of press releases from business all over the country" and is thus an invaluable index and guide to the relative significance of events. And the *Journal* has maintained the top investigative staff in this field.[29]

NEWS BOUGHT AND SHARED: THE WIRE SERVICES

The growth of newspapers in the colonial days of America and the intense competition between those newspapers, especially for news from overseas (which arrived only by ship), gave rise to a system of shared, or "pooled" coverage. By this means, newspapers pooled their resources. They agreed to send one correspondent out to meet an arriving ship to get the European newspapers and interview the captain and officers for other items of interest, and then to speed to shore in a launch with the news. This information would then be carried on horseback (or, later, telegraphed) to the newspapers who had purchased the service. This was the beginning of the wire services in the United States. Thus, before the American colonies had their freedom, the American mass media system was emerging.

Today, newspapers share news under a similar, though vastly more sophisticated, system. Wire services, as well as newspaper syndicates, send stories via leased wire into the newsrooms all over the country.

Stories transmitted by wire may be trimmed down from their original length, or rewritten to make them universally acceptable to the variety of editorial tastes and needs. The need for uniform style and grammar sometimes takes the punch and color out of wire service stories, and editors complain about the dryness of wire copy, but seldom does wire service copy reflect any bias.

The major independent wire services, The Associated Press, United Press International, and Dow Jones in the United States, and Reuters in Europe, feed almost all the nation's newspapers and broadcast stations. It is a vast and powerful business. The Associated Press serves 3500 radio stations; Dow Jones serves 116; UPI counts 5881 subscribers; almost all of the 1760 newspapers in the country receive at least one or more major news wire. The AP has 119 domestic and 66 foreign bureaus. UPI has 99 domestic and 62 foreign news bureaus.[30]

With the advent of radio, the major independent wire services began preparing radio copy in a sportier, breezier, chattier style, without conforming to the stricter rules of print journalism. This service has made it possible for a low-budget radio station to take news directly off the teletype, and compete with larger stations for the same news audience.

The New York Times, The Los Angeles Times, Newsweek, and *The Washington Post,* and other newspapers have adopted similar services to "sell" their national stories. They maintain large staffs in major world capitals. The dependence of small papers upon newspaper wire services has, of course, enhanced the importance and influence of the major newspapers. About 400 newspapers around the country now subscribe to *The New York Times'* wire service.

Subscribers to a major print and broadcast service are likely to receive not only the major national trunk line, called the "A" wire by some, but also a number of other wires. For instance, the subscription may include a secondary national wire, with stories of lesser or regional importance, a statewide wire, for stories of statewide interest only, a financial wire, which carries only business and financial news during the day, and may be converted to a racing wire at night, and a sports wire, which carries only news of sports and racing results.

The wire services operate on 12-hour "cycles" in order to serve the needs of subscribers best. The cycles begin at 1 A.M. and at 1 P.M. and enable the services to meet the deadline demands of morning and afternoon newspapers. The news stories are completely rewritten and updated at the beginning of each cycle. Wire service offices are usually staffed and operational 24 hours a day, seven days a week, to meet the continuing demands from all types of print and broadcast subscribers for fresh news. Wire service bureaus are located in all state capitals and in most major cities and capitals of the world. Often, only one or two persons will staff a bureau, though hundreds may be working in such major cities as New York and Washington. Most of the work of wire service reporters, particularly in bureaus outside Washington and New York, involves condensing and rewriting news that appears in the publications or on the broadcasts of stations in which they are located. The primary operational rule for all of them, however, has been expressed by Dorothy Brooks, of United Press International:

> We shouldn't be just fast and accurate, but we should be brief. There is tremendous competition for this budget of space. The wire services operate within budgets: financial budgets, time budgets and space budgets, and their resources are not open-ended. They are not the *Federal Register*—everything cannot be thrown in there.[31]

Since there is such competition for attention, informal rules have been adopted by each of the major services for inclusion of business news on the daily summaries. Normally business stories at the end of a quarter involving companies with earnings of $100 million or more are included. (Sometimes the size of a company is measured only by the exchange on which it is listed.) The size of a transaction may determine whether or not it is reported. At Dow Jones, which publishes *The Wall Street Journal*, any transaction under $5 million must be unusual in character to be deemed newsworthy. With respect to personalities in the news, usually only job changes of the top two officers of the 500 largest companies are mentioned.

CHAPTER 4

News and Business: Media Shortcomings

Question: Mr. Young, I'm curious. How thick-skinned or thin-skinned are journalists with respect to criticism?
Mr. Young: They are the worst of all.

Louis H. Young, Editor, Business Week.

Business complains that reporters are economically illiterate, that business news gets inadequate coverage; the media fosters an antibusiness bias; reports on business profits are misleading; and media personnel in general are incapable of providing fair analysis or a perspective on business developments.

ECONOMIC ILLITERACY

Much business reporting is "flawed by errors of fact, interpretation and judgment that would embarrass even an undergraduate economics major," contends James R. Shepley, president of Time, Inc. Local business reporting, he says, is often superficial and may amount to less than half of the total space devoted to sports.[1]

A beginning reporter may be asked to handle an incredible diversity of assignments. As a result, too many general assignment reporters are ill-equipped for the specificities good business reporting demands. The classical, perhaps apocryphal, story making the rounds at business luncheon tables concerns the story of the young reporter who called on a *Fortune* 500 chief executive officer—and revealed that he did not know the difference between stocks and bonds. As we saw in Chapter 1, nothing in the formal training of journalism students ensures that they will know anything about how to read a balance sheet, or translate M1 into a meaningful term for the average reader, or, for that matter, know the difference between stocks and bonds. In emphasizing the parochial skills of the trade, such as layout, design technique, headline writing, the law pertaining to the press, and history of the press, journalism schools by and large fail to leave enough time for students to learn enough about any particular field to do an adequate job of reporting. As a result, journalists remain not only economically illiterate, but also, for example, artistically and politically illiterate. Perhaps the successful journalist of the future would do well to major in some scientific or literary discipline and acquire the tools of the journalism profession as one of several minor fields of study.

In addition, journalists are often impatient, looking for easy-to-condense stories. There is more than a kernel of truth in the cartoon in which a TV news director is berating the new anchor man, "What's the matter, Figsby? You went to journalism school. Why can't you sum up the world situation in 30-seconds?" In addition, journalists see themselves primarily as skeptics, adversaries, and always on the alert for misbehavior. When a complicated story breaks requiring research and reasoning, they are both unwilling and incapable of giving it much play or attention. Take the case of the energy crisis, brought dramatically to the nation's attention by the oil embargo, long lines at gasoline stations, and sharply higher prices. It was a crisis not only for the government, but has also proved too large for the news media to handle.

"The news coverage of the embargo was a horrendous experience," recalls Alton W. Whitehouse, chairman of Standard Oil of Ohio.[2] William Simon, formerly head of the Federal Energy Administration said:

> These charges surged through the network news mechanisms and flooded the country with paranoid suspicions, after which the newsmen dashed around, collecting the feedback from citizens who repeated the suspicions as fact, and retransmitted them over the air waves. Vastly more coverage was given to the false rumors than to the actual facts of the shortage.[3]

SOHIO's Whitehouse says: "It was an example of reporters not having the faintest notion of what they were reporting." However, he adds, in fairness to the press, that businessmen "were deficient in not considering how important it is to help the press get the real facts. We were unresponsive and, by God, we learned that we were wrong."[4]

Louis Banks of the Massachusetts Institute of Technology, a former editor of *Fortune*, says:

> We are fed a daily diet of authoritative ignorance, most of which conveys a cheap-shot hostility to business and businessmen. The

nation sees a persistently distorted image of its most productive and pervasive activity, business. . . . The reporters and editors in the general media are woefully ignorant of the complexities and ambiguities of corporate operations, and being so, are easy targets for politicians or pressure group partisans with special axes to grind at the expense of business.[5]

BIAS IN THE MEDIA

A nationwide survey conducted through the University of Texas found that 84.6 percent of those responding believed that journalists slant the news, and 71.6 percent of the journalists agreed.[6] This finding was supported not long ago by media critic Edith Efron who conducted an experiment, denying herself access for two weeks to all sources of news except television. At the end of the period she drew several conclusions about television's view of the American system of capitalism:

1. American big businessmen are cheats, liars, and bribers, whose greed is limitless and who make gigantic profits;
2. American industry is a lethal institution that is poisoning our air, water, and soil and is infecting us all with cancer.[7]

Indeed, it has become almost an article of faith among businessmen that bias exists in the media. The prevailing sentiment seems that held by John Brooks, writing in the journalism magazine *The Quill:*

Many a young reporter is straining to make his reputation and his fortune by "getting the goods" on a corporation or a businessman. If the goods aren't there, or if he lacks the talent or competence to find them, innuendo will do. Unfortunately, it will often do for his editor also—provided, of course, that the subject isn't an important advertiser.[8]

That view does not seem to be limited to outsiders. The late "NBC Evening News" anchor man, Chet Huntley, after his last broadcast, and upon becoming a business entrepreneur himself, wrote in *The Wall Street Journal:* "One general characteritic of the American press which seems inexplicable to me is the basic antipathy towards business and industry which I believe exists in journalists." [9] Supporting Huntley's view is Lew Young, editor of *Business* Week. While discussing newspapermen who like to think they are very liberal, he said:

They think that one of the marks of being liberal is to show anti-business bias. It starts with a feeling that business is probably not good. . . . that business is prepared to do anything to make a profit. This is re-emphasized by a lack of understanding of how business works by newspaper reporters, since most have never worked in a business.[10]

Most reporters, however, are "just trying to do their job," in the words of James R. Shepley, president of *Time.* "It's not bias that is producing almost daily reports of corporations caught making bribes to foreign officials to win contracts." [11] His counterpart at *Newsweek,* Osborne Elliott, says there is no antibusiness bias, "conscious or unconscious" at *Newsweek,* "but there certainly is an anti-crooked business bias." [12]

What business people are generally referring to as bias may in actuality be lack of objectivity, or it may be superficiality, in reporting. "The very decisions about what news to cover, what prominence to give it, and what kind of follow-up to accord it require a process of deliberate selectivity based on the subjective assessment of an editor as to what is relevant and important for the audience." Objectivity, however, is a relative term.

HEADLINES

Headlines frequently give a distorted view of a story's meaning and are a constant source of frustration to serious readers as well as to newsmakers. However, headlines also help newspapers sell their product. Besides summarizing a story in a few words, headlines, written to whet the reader's appetite, provide an index for the newspaper and make for better organization of the pages. At most newspapers, headlines are never written by the reporter who wrote or covered a story but rather by an editor. The headline, itself a summary, is written on the summary of the story in the lead paragraph. The language and words, known as "telegraph sentences" convey the general idea of the story. When implicit or explicit distortion creeps into a headline, it may be that the story itself is distorted, or that the headline is an oversimplification of the lead paragraph.

REPORTING ON PROFITS

For many years, advertisements have been aimed at attracting new business to various states. As an example, "Profit is not a dirty word in Ohio." The implication has been made that restrictive legislation would not be imposed on businesses and that business would not be attacked for success.

Senator Henry Jackson, chairman of the Senate Energy Committee, won headlines by charging that oil company profits were "obscene"—a word that encapsulated the popular belief that big is bad. So successfully did that phrase summarize popular suspicions that many people today will agree that the profits of the energy industry are "obscene." William Simon, commenting on a study of profits, which employed data covering the period from 1958 through 1973, writes:

> The petroleum industry ranked in the middle range of the 29 industries studied. At the highest end of the scale were instruments and metal products; printing, publishing and television industries; and big lumber, with respective profit growth rates of 17.3, 15.3, and 14.7, respectively. At the lowest end of the scale, ranked 29th, was iron and steel, which had a profit growth rate of 1.4 percent over a fifteen-year period.[13]

A later study, done in 1977 by Warren Brookes of the Boston Herald-American, updated the FTC-Treasury figures. Brookes compared the profits of the communication conglomerates with those of other industries. He discovered that between 1973 and 1975, pre-tax profits for food retailers were 1.3 percent of sales; for the oil industries, 8.2 percent, and for the television industry, 19.1 percent.

Simon, noting the irony, says,

> The worst barrage of oil company demogoguery has come over the network air. Reporters [have] transmitted the liberal Congressmen's canards about oil company profits without even bothering to check on the profits of their own industry, which are more than twice as great.[14]

Adding to the problem of accurately reporting on profits is the fact that business reports profits in different ways for different audiences. Business wants to assure the investing public that its own profits are attractive. Therefore, in statements directed to investors, a firm whose earnings increased from one to two pennies per dollar of sales, is likely to announce, "Profits were up 200 percent in the quarter just ended. . . ." But in announcements to the news media, a company may play down the higher-looking number, reporting from the same data, "Profits increased one cent in the quarter ended. . . ."

This actually was the case, for a Boston supermarket chain complained that *The Boston Globe* had headlined that its profits were "up 200 percent" at a time when consumers were very upset about supermarket food prices. The truth is that the chain was recovering from a *loss* the previous year, and was earning, overall, less than 1 percent after taxes on gross revenues.[15]

NO MEANINGFUL YARDSTICK

The news media and the business community would do well to arrive at some uniform measure when reporting on profits. For instance, it might be best to measure profits in cents per dollar of sales, or in earnings per share. Whatever standard is adopted, it should not resemble the one widely in use now: profit as a percentage increase or decrease over the previous period's figures. This measure is simply subject to too much confusion and misinterpretation.

Richard Cheney of Hill and Knowlton, has written, "This is the problem for reporters in writing about earnings, 'Are they really writing about something, or is it a myth?" Basing profits on earnings may perform a great disservice by misleading society as to its economic well-being, he says: "It's like a ship using a fathometer that is incorrect, but one that everyone has agreed to use. Some day the ship may end up on the shoals while the meter shows that the ship is in 50 feet of water." [16]

William Wendel, president of Carborundum, acknowledges industry's "propensity to brag about increased earnings over the previous years," and suggests that the emphasis "should be on earnings as a percentage of sales." [17]

FAIR ANALYSIS

Public misunderstanding of the extent of profits has been dismal for a long time. Polls taken more than 40 years ago showed that most people believed that business was profiting at a rate of about 25 cents for every dollar of revenue. A recent survey found that high-school students estimated that the average profit of an American business on a dollar of sales was 30 cents. College students estimated it was 45 cents. The truth is that the average profit is a little more than a nickel. "Where would students get ideas like that?" asked Frank Shakespeare in an address delivered at New York University's Media 78 Conference. "They aren't taught it at home; they're not really taught it in high school or colleges, even though there might be some anti-business bias in some pedagogical institutions, and they don't read the business pages of newspapers." Shakespeare suggests that television is to blame:

> When television covers new profits, it covers the abnormal amount, the atypical, and they say that General Motors profits were up 78 percent, or the oil companies were up 63 percent, or they use a money figure—$900 million in profits for AT&T sounds like a staggering amount.
>
> What they're really talking about is that profits went from a nickel to six-and-a-half cents on the sales dollar. That's lost in the translation. What gets reported is that profits quarter-to-quarter went up 61 percent to $47 million, and that's sort of a "Wow-Gee" figure.[18]

The great majority of the public—90 percent, according to some polls—accepts profits as necessary as long as they make producing goods and services possible. That is, profits are the source of new capital and equipment, raw materials, and components to produce items for sale. In short, says John Steiner, in *Business Horizons,* "Profits are used to maintain the viability of a business which includes, of course, assuring jobs. These aspects of profits should be pointed out at every opportunity." [19] This is important to emphasize because the public largely deplores what it considers to be profiteering and the distinction between legitimate profit and profiteering is unclear, except in the extremes. As a result, profits, especially aggregate profits of any amount, are frequently attacked. President Carter's inflation advisor warned publicly in mid-1979 that the growth of corporate profits "puts business on trial in the eyes of the American people." Publisher Malcolm Forbes made a rebuttal on behalf of business:

> People see in headlines and hear on TV percentage-profit highs at the same time they are reading and hearing of inflation raging toward new records. And naturally, they relate the two.
>
> Who's to understand, who's to bother explaining that these first-quarter profits are percentagely high only vis à vis the same quarter a year ago? Remember a year ago? In the first three months of 1978 our economy was hobbled by the worst-ever winter in many areas, by the longest coal strike in our history, by factory-shutting power shortages. Then *this* first quarter was hyped by stockpiling in anticipation of the expiration of trucking and other labor contracts, and by balance-sheet adrenaline from foreign currency adjustments to a

dollar that also turned up when OPEC tightened its grip on our oil jugular.

None of which has a blamed thing to do with profiteering or the relation of profits to the rate of inflation.[20]

CHAPTER 5

The News Business

As a society, we have developed an almost insatiable appetite for news. Yet, we seem to prefer it in short, convenient servings, and television and radio, as a result, provide only headline service. We may wonder what news really is, who decides what is news, and whether what one hears is either true or important to know.

NEWS

Trying to define what is news is difficult because news is so often ephemeral. Any definition today may become invalid tomorrow, when different elements become more important. Thus, consequence and timing are key elements. If an item does not affect a great number of people in a significant way over a lengthy period of time—or is not highly unusual—then it may never be considered news at all.

Some journalists suggest that the essence of news is confrontation, the clashing of opposing forces. Edward R. Murrow said news was the abnormality of society. E. R. Kane, president of DuPont, says he has learned that "only aberrations from general expectations are considered newsworthy." [1] Tom Brokaw of NBC's "Today Show" says news is change "as reported by an outsider. And since change is seldom a comforting situation in our lives in whatever form it takes, news takes on a sinister meaning. It is not simply "news"—it is "bad news." [2]

George Heinemann, a vice president of NBC, explains, in contrast, that, "When it is something you like, it is news. When it is something you don't like or your boss doesn't like, it's propaganda." [3] To complicate the definition, it must be remembered that news which looks "bad" to one individual looks "good" to another. Just as, for example, the potential buyer and the potential seller of a stock take differing views of changes in that stock's price, so the reporter and the executive may view the same incident as a "bad" or "good" story.

Perhaps the press is unloved in the business community today for reasons proposed by businessman John deButts, former chairman of American Telephone and Telegraph. He notes that the press "is less likely to cover business developments than it is business problems." [4] Sophocles summed up the reason in 450 B.C.: "None loves the messenger who brings bad news."

A noble case can be made that the press has an obligation to help business and the public understand one another, yet not every journalist admits that as a priority objective. The news media view it as their purpose to "balance" any story by seeking contrasting sources or angles, as well as to sample or rearrange a news release. It may be argued that balancing a story eventually works for the protection of the public, but the practice of "balancing" every statement with a contrasting view also may raise doubts about the validity of every public pronouncement.

JOURNALISTIC TRAINING

There is no certification program to license a person as a bona fide journalist the way there is to accredit accountants, attorneys, or barbers. Those who want to write, can do so. If their writing is adequate, an editor may hire them. College credentials may help, but they are not required. The main characteristics of a reporter are patience, persistence, imagination, vocabulary, and a rough conformity to style.

Journalists attend school primarily to develop these characteristics and skills rather than to develop analytical abilities. For this reason, American newspapers have been attacked by Irving Kristol. The journalist need not know anything about any of the several subjects on which he reports. He need only know the principles of reporting itself, no matter whether it's "a case of a one-alarm fire or a 12-alarm revolution."

Colleges do not require that journalism students choose a major in a field of academic interest, such as the arts, politics, or business, with a specified number of courses taken in the academic discipline and a specified number in journalism. Thus, reporters pride themselves on being, as *Washington Post* publisher Katherine Graham calls them, "professional laymen." Not surprisingly, then, some of the top financial publications refuse to draw their talent from the pool of "trained" journalists. At *The Wall Street Journal,* the pattern has been to hire people "usually with very little experience and train them ourselves in our own discipline. We have historically looked for people with a generalist background," says Robert Bartley, editor of the editorial page. "A degree in economics, for instance, would probably be a negative factor, because it has been our experience that it's very difficult to teach those people to write. Our trend is hiring people with somewhat more education. I hired my second Ph.D. in the last few months, and we have some MBAs working for us now in the news department." [5] Further, Robert Flaherty was one of two MBAs hired by *Forbes* magazine in 1961, just after graduating from Harvard. "Now we are flooded with Ph.d.s, lawyers, and all these kind of people, and I think the training of people coming in is superb." [6]

Publisher Katherine Graham of *The Washington Post* says:

> We usually do not hire "experts" because the reporter who is expert in wheat marketing doesn't know anything about the oil business. The expert on oil doesn't necessarily know anything about automobile production, or international monetary policy. But a reporter, in the course of a week's work, may have to write about all of them.[7]

In Graham's view, that is the way it should be; in the view of those who are being written about, it is not. Economic philosopher Irving Kristol takes issue with Graham's view of journalistic training:

> American journalism is rapidly becoming an underdeveloped profession—its methods anachronistic, its habits injurious, its sloth impenetrable. Every year, the American journalist becomes relatively more ignorant—relative to the complexity of the subject matter, the accumulated knowledge about this subject matter, and the increasing number of his readers who have a genuine, professional connection with the subject matter.

Kristol charges that behind the basic directives issued to reporters, "Get it right" and "Tell it straight" lies a primordial assumption: "All news is of one substance—only the magnitude differs. And this assumption has an equally firm corollary: There is such a thing as journalistic expertise that renders superfluous any true expert knowledge. Upon these twin rocks American journalism lies impaled, like a floundering whale." [8] Kristol suggests that more journalists should receive academic training in some specialty, with at least contextual and perhaps theoretical knowledge of their subject matter. Kristol offers this test:

The New York Times Washington Bureau has over 25 reporters, each a supposed, if temporary, "specialist"—two covering the White House, three the State Department, four the Congress, and so on. Let us say that someone wanted to edit a book of ten essays to be used by the college student of American government and politics, covering such Washington institutions as the Pentagon, the Supreme Court, Congress, the administrative agencies, etc. Would one think instinctively of asking *The New York Times* man to contribute? Would one even know his name? These questions pretty much answer themselves. Now this is really odd, I submit. A great newspaper should be able to make a better showing than this.[9]

As a result of this kind of criticism, the press is finally starting to realize the depths of its own ignorance. Understanding the energy crisis, for instance, which is almost constantly in the news these days, demands, at the least, knowledge of the coal, oil, gas and uranium industries and their interconnections and the relative economics of producing synthetic oil from coal or shale. It requires a knowledge of international politics and the domestic political processes, including the role of various federal regulatory agencies. Consequently, many business and financial editors fear that the complexities of their assignments are quickly outpacing their abilities to gather and analyze information.

CHAPTER 6

Public Affairs

Corporate expectations of public relations departments or agencies have grown as rapidly during the past decade as have the demands upon the corporation. Much of the responsibility for the new role for conveying a favorable image of corporations to society has been placed in the hands of communications and public affairs departments. Yet those involved with public relations not only face opposition from top management, but also rejection from those to whom they are attempting to communicate on the outside. Management may complain that public relations is a costly and nonproductive exercise and that it is unnecessary in a well-managed company. The public may complain. A large utility recently was asked, "Why don't you drop your advertising, stop trying to communicate with the public, and pass on to your customers the resultant savings?" [1]

In recent years, however, management and the public have slowly grown to recognize that there are important reasons to maintain a public affairs department. As early as 1934, concern was expressed that corporate silence could have an impact upon honest and fair securities transactions. That year saw passage of the Securities Exchange Act, aimed at protecting the investing public. Disclosure regulations hinge on the principle that "material events" must be disclosed immediately by publicly held companies. Whether the news be bad or good, public affairs departments have, more and more, been given the responsibility to make it available to the investing public.

In the near future, the public affairs director is more likely to be part of management councils where important decisions are made. For, in the public corporation, every major decision has some impact on the public. In the words of one expert:

The bigger the decision, the larger the company, and the greater the number of people that are affected, the more significant the PR component becomes. More often than not, however, the chief executive officer would no more consult with PR about a major policy matter than ask his barber for stock market investment advice. And yet major public relations problems continually arise from policy decisions in which PR has had no part.[2]

Indeed, the public affairs officer should become more a part of management, not simply a tool of management.

Today, the modern public affairs office must do more than perform the traditional functions of public relations: product publicity, fielding press inquiries, writing executives' speeches, writing annual reports and brochures, editing the house organ for employees, and coordinating community projects for the firm. Dealing with financial and security analysts, seeking and creating opportunities for executives to speak, and aggressively selling top management to the media (and vice versa) are some of the additional functions assumed by public affairs offices.

In addition, the public affairs director must sometimes act as an "outsider in the executive suite," as one analyst put it, advising management on the various perspectives of external constituencies: "The PR director must view corporate policies with multiple vision to an extent that is not done by any other staff officer. For those in PR, loyalty to the company is never an excuse for failure to observe it from every point of view, including the most hostile, actual or potential." [3]

William A. Durbin, chairman of Hill & Knowlton, the public relations agency, has predicted that "The PR function is about to cross the threshold from a primarily communications function to a management function participating systematically in the formation of policy and the decision-making process itself." [4] Unfortunately, not all managers agree with that assessment. They believe that public affairs officers do not have the skills and the managerial know-how to participate in high-level decision-making. About 60 percent of the chief executives who responded to a questionnaire by consultant W. Howard Chase declared that they had no confidence in their public affairs officers.[5] This lack of confidence may be due to the fact that the product of public relations is not usually quantifiable, and management likes to assess results in those terms.[6] Despite the widespread lack of faith in public relations, the time has arrived for business to make the same types of nonproductive expenditures for communications purposes that it has for pollution abatement.[7]

On the external side, public affairs has a long way to go before its practitioners get where they think they should be. (Asked to rank 16 professions and occupations in terms of their respect for each, journalists ranked themselves first, and ranked public relations people last in the group of 16.) In turn, the public relations practitioners, however, and not surprisingly, ranked journalists third and themselves fourth (first and second were physicians and architects). Public relations people ranked politicians last, while journalists ranked politicians 15th—only one place above PR people.[8] Unsophisticated public affairs counselors who distrust journalists advise clients to keep their heads in the sand, to be unavailable for comment, to avoid reality and to contribute by silence to general misunderstanding and misinformation about business." As a result some journalists, like Sylvia Chase, have objected to the policy of relying upon public relations people instead of managers for their stories: "What you really want to do is talk to the president of the company. Why do you want to do that? Because these are the people who run corporations. Public relations people don't run them." [10] Tom Brokaw, who has dealt with numerous public relations people, has said:

> Most businesses, in my view, have a public relations man who doesn't really count. He's not as important as divisional vice presidents, he doesn't get paid enough, he's not first class. There should be a whole upgrading of the top public relations officer in big corporate business. He should be one of the principal executives, top paid and in on everything, whether they want it or not is irrelevant. It is necessary in order to relate to the communications revolution. . . . With rare exceptions like Herb Schmertz—Mobil is a classic example of a brilliant move—They take a man, they pay him a pile of money, he's clearly at the top, involved in the policy, and when he speaks you know that he knows everything about Mobil. Mobil is getting superb press because they're tough and because they handle it right. . . .[11]

Reg Laite, News Director of WOR Radio, reiterated Brokaw's remarks but has pointed out that:

> I'm a newsman who loves *competent* PR men, and I emphasize competent because what happens in industrial America is you go out and hire someone for the cheapest bucks, you put him in a cubicle somewhere, you give him a broken-down typewriter and a bunch of paper, and say okay, represent. The best PR men work for the best companies of America. I'm talking about New York Telephone Company, and General Tire. . . . They're given the confidence of the

company and they work on a first name basis with the chairman of the board. They meet with him on a regular basis.[12]

Rob Sunde of WCBS Radio concurred, and added: "There are a handful [of public relations people] that I trust implicitly—that have developed trust through competence—and we have a very symbiotic relationship."

CHAPTER 7

Advertising

If business sometimes regards the news media as its natural adversary, then it is an ironic commentary that business has for so long subsidized newspapers, radio, and television through advertising. Advertising is the one area where business and media have traditionally cooperated with one another, either by choice or out of recognition of their interdependence. In recent years, they have even joined forces to fight the increasing amount of government intervention in this area. Advertising has become, as a result, the bridge between opponents on each side of the conflict between business and the media.

By definition, advertising is "the paid dissemination of information for the purpose of selling or helping to sell commodities and services or gaining the acceptance of ideas that may cause people to think or act in a certain way." [1] In the broadest sense, advertising is a synthesis of business and communication. In effect, it is a spinoff of business: Media is the means to achieve an economic goal.

AGENCIES AND BIG BUSINESS

There is no question that advertising is business; it is big business. The industry has experienced considerable growth in the last 20 years, and there is likely to be a movement toward "super" advertising agencies in the eighties as consolidation continues and marketing becomes as important as finance in traditionally nonmarketing companies.

Figures from the Aspen Institute show that in the United States the amount of money spent on newspaper advertising grew 169 percent, radio advertising 229 percent, and television advertising 313 percent for the 16-year period from 1960 to 1976. Although it is doubtful that the growth will continue at these rates, especially with respect to television advertising, money spent on advertising will continue to increase overall. In the sixties the annual advertising budget for McDonald's Hamburgers was \$5,000,000. The figure was increased to over \$20,000,000 in the seventies.

In spite of the growth of advertising, the business community often regards advertisers as an unwelcome partner, and a necessary evil. Because they do not understand the techniques and intracacies of advertising, managers fear they may become the victims of an agency trying to increase "billings." In addition, some journalists express outright contempt for their advertising counterparts, who often began their careers in print or broadcast media, and like public relations personnel, are regarded as the "high priced cousins" who have left the more noble profession of news and sold-out to business.

HISTORY

There is no specific point when advertising, as we think of it today, became part of the marketing function. Word of mouth is probably its oldest form. Like merchants in the open markets and street peddlers now, businessmen in ancient times tried various means to attract customers for their services or wares. The volcanic ruins of Pompeii have preserved examples of Roman advertising. Outside stores, pictures or symbols were hung on placards advertising the commodity or service offered within, and written advertisements were carved into stone or terracotta and set into walls or hung in brackets. For example, one old sign reads, "To rent, from the first day of next July, shops . . . finer upper chambers and a house in the Arius Pollio block, owned by Gnaeus Marius." [2]

Between the sixth and fifteenth centuries, there is little evidence of what, if any, system of advertising existed beyond those introduced earlier. Then, Gutenberg revolutionized communication by introducing moveable type. The printing press contributed to increased literacy as a result of the production of books and the printing of periodical publications. During the next two centuries, print advertising grew rapidly. Unfortunately, not all of the ads were totally truthful. The advertising copy for Dr. Ryan's Sugar Plumbs is a case in point. The Plumbs were proclaimed to be a cure for: "Paleness of the Face, Itching of the Nose, Hollowness of the Eyes, Grating of the teeth when asleep, Dullness, Pains, and Heaviness in the Head, a dry Cough, an Itching in the Fundament, white and thick Urine, unquiet Sleep, often starting, lost appetite, swell'd Belly, Gnawing and Biting about the stomach, frightful Dreams, extreme Thirsts, the Body decay'd lean, Fits, often Vomiting, stinking Breath." [3]

By middle of the next century, manufacturers and retailers of all products "generally thought that the only way to convince the public was to overstate their case—and the belief is not dead yet." [4] As a result, business managers came to realize the tremendous power of advertising, but consumers learned to take everything with a grain of salt.

A new medium revolutionized communications and the advertising industry when Guglielmo Marconi sent the first wireless electronic signal across the Atlantic Ocean in 1901. Of course, neither Marconi nor anyone connected with the first days of radio ever thought it would become commercial or profitable. General Electric, Westinghouse, and the Radio Corporation of America—the major manufacturers of radio receivers—built and operated the first radio stations with revenues from the sales of their new receivers. When it became evident that the revenues were not covering their rising costs, the industry rejected proposals for such as a government supported system. Instead, they began to sell time for commercial use as was the practice in the newspaper and magazine industries. 1927 was the first full year of operation of permanent commercial radio networks. Then, in 1939 commercial television became a reality, and in 1941 WNBT (now WNBC-TV) in New York began broadcasting with four commercial sponsors.[5] Television readily adopted the structure and format of radio. From the beginning, advertising was recognized as the source of sponsorship and revenues.

ADVERTISING STANDS ALONE

The separation of news and entertainment from the advertising function is maintained by the organizational structure of media companies, perhaps as a carryover from past practice. Thus, editorial and advertising departments usually coexist with little or no interaction. Journalism texts and schools tend to perpetuate the division on the basis that "editorial gathers and prepares the news" while advertising "solicits and prepares the commercial message." [6] Almost everyone who has worked in a newsroom has a story about a news editor throwing an ad man out of the office for trying to promote or prevent a story about an advertiser. Thus, "Journalists tend to project their perception of media content categories to the audience. It is assumed that the audience clearly distinguishes between the advertising and nonadvertising content of the media and . . .

like journalists, considers advertising as a homogeneous concept across media." [7]

CREDIBILITY OF ADVERTISING

There is a surprising lack of information disseminated about audience perception of and belief in advertising in the various media. The studies which have been conducted indicate that audiences trust or accept advertising to different degrees depending on the medium. The result of one study revealed that newspaper readers do not distinguish between "advertising" and "news" if the content contains information considered to be of value to them. That is, both advertising and news are apparently regarded as "information," especially if the advertisement is in small, local newspapers. People in the sample perceived television primarily as a source of entertainment. They liked television news programs, but disliked television commercials.[8]

The credibility of advertising in all the media was measured in several studies which suggest that, while attitudes depend on factors such as age and education level, the general reaction of people is that newspaper ads are perceived to be more trustworthy than those on either TV or radio, except among younger subjects who are more positive about television.[9] The weaknesses of advertising must be recognized. As Thomas Murphy, Chairman of General Motors points out: "to communicate with a skeptical public we lean heavily on advertising, the easy medium, but unfortunately one that has credibility problems of its own." [10]

DEFENDERS AND CRITICS

The use of television and radio advertising does offer an advantage. This advantage can best be explained by the fact that "broadcasting advertising is virtually inescapable. Printed advertising, whether by mail, bill board, magazine, or newspaper can be ignored. But broadcast advertising occurs in the stream of whatever is attracting our attention on radio or television. It interrupts, intrudes, and consequently is almost unavoidably annoying." [11] That, of course, is the value of television advertising, as well as its disadvantage.

Advocates also point to economic theory to support the practice and concept of advertising:

Advertising performs a useful, and probably indispensable, economic function as the cheapest and most efficient method for establishing the connection between mass production and the mass of consumers. It also performs an invaluable social function in providing support and independence to news media of all kinds, including broadcasting, newspapers, magazines, and academic and technical publications.[12]

However, some people are critical of advertising because it can be misleading and, therefore, can lead to inefficient allocation of resources.

Thus, a study by Professors Bauer and Greyse, found that 26 percent of the respondents to a consumer survey cited advertisements as annoying or offensive on "information failure" grounds.[13] In addition, a New York advertising agency found that 60 percent of a sample group surveyed believed that less than half of all advertising is honest and informative.[14] The records of the Federal Trade Commission's rulemaking proceedings, concerned with whether advertising provides honest product information uphold this sentiment. In areas such as gasoline octane ratings, wattage of stereo equipment, and labeling of detergent ingredients the records are replete with testimony as to the dishonesty of the statements made in advertisements.

Lee Loevinger, a former Chairman of the FTC, has offered four reasons for the criticism of advertising.

1. Much criticism of advertising is an exercise in hostility arising from the general antibusiness bias, which is part of the overall loss of confidence in institutions.
2. There is more advertising than ever before and it is more noticeable. Advertising has increased in proportion to the GNP, not the population. Since the end of World War II, the population of the United States has increased about 50 percent, while GNP has increased over 370 percent.
3. People have become aware of genuine advertising abuses, including "bald misrepresentations, exaggerations, boring repetition, tasteless and offensive depictions and appeals."
4. The Federal Trade Commission has criticized the advertising industry, perhaps in an attempt to gain control over it and thus more power. "It is natural and inevitable that the FTC should see advertising as an irresistably alluring field for the expansion of its power and appropriations because an attack on broadcast advertising is a sure way of winning public attention. . . . Furthermore, broadcasting is vulnerable because of its licensed status." [15]

Others, like Galbraith, oppose the purpose and concept of advertising itself:

> The protective purpose of going beyond prices to influence consumer response is to prevent the defection of consumers which thus would plunge the firm into a loss. The affirmative purpose is, of course, to recruit new customers and thus to expand sales—to serve the goal of growth. . . . The advertising of one individual automobile company seeks to win consumers from other makers. But the advertising of all together contributes to the conviction that happiness is associated with automobile ownership. The result is a control of consumer reactions, which, though imperfect and greatly complicated by the rival, is still far more secure than would be the ungoverned responses of consumers in the absence of such efforts.[16]

Said Milton Marcus, vice president, Claire Advertising Agency: "The quality of life in a society is determined by the quality of its culture. Ours is rotten. The advertising industry has helped create it and is continuing to make it worse." [17]

GOVERNMENT AND ADVERTISING

Government became concerned with advertising practices during the last century when, as discussed earlier, abuses in advertising became obvious. Miles Kirkpatrick, another former FTC chairman, explains the philosophy and logic behind the government's policy:

> As the experience of the late 19th Century in this country demonstrated, the consequence of an unbridled competitive system—one in which competitors are free to employ unfair, coercive and collusive tactics—was increasing monopoly. As a result of that experience, the need for legislation designed to ban anti-competitive practices in the marketplace became evident.[18]

When the Sherman Act of 1890 passed, advertising was believed to be one of the monopolistic practices in constraint of trade. Traditionally, those favoring regulation give the following explanation to support their belief. Once an industry becomes monopolized, whether by a single firm or a cartel, a heavy advertising campaign is often undertaken for the purpose of eliminating possible competition. However, the monopolization of an industry is conducive to deceptive advertising for two reasons.

For one, the customer cannot retaliate even if he discovers the fraud because there is no close substitute for the product, and, secondly, there is little incentive for whatever competitors there are to combat false claims.

Initially, monopoly growth waned after 1890; however, the wording of the Sherman Antitrust Act was too general to permit the courts to enforce the provisions of the Act, such as honest advertising. The Clayton Act was passed in 1914 and the Federal Trade Commission was created to enforce antitrust activities. The FTC is an independent federal regulatory agency with the authority to study business behavior and to prevent practices which could threaten the competitive system and those which are unfair and deceptive to the consuming public.

Within the FTC, major responsibility for combating false advertising rests with the Bureau of Deceptive Practices.

THE FEDERAL TRADE COMMISSION

Section 54 of the Federal Trade Commission Act requires that advertisers refrain from deception in advertising and declares that dissemination of false advertising is an unfair or deceptive act or practice. To enforce this prohibition, the FTC was empowered to issue cease and desist orders. Once again, however, the vague wording in Section 5 made enforcement difficult.

In many of its early cases the Federal Trade Commission had little support from the courts. For example, the FTC challenged the Raladam Company, which had claimed that its product "Marmola" was the cure for obesity. Speaking for the Court, Justice Sutherland ruled in 1931 that Section 5 of the FTC Act did not forbid the deception of consumers and disallowed the FTC's order that the Raladam Company cease such advertising. However, the Commission won a significant victory in 1938, when Congress passed the Wheeler-Lea Amendments, which gave the Commission punitive powers and required that a company cease and desist disseminating false and misleading information, defined as:

... not only representations made or suggested by statement, word, design, device, or sound, or any combination thereof, but also the extent to which advertising fails to reveal facts material in the light of such representation or material with respect to consequences which may result from the use of the commodity prescribed in said advertisement or under such conditions as are customary or usual.

The Amendment to Section 45 of the FTC Act reads "Unfair methods of competition in commerce, and unfair or deceptive acts or practices in commerce are hereby declared unlawful. . . ." Section 52 (1) states: "It shall be unlawful for any person, partnership, or corporation to disseminate, or cause to be disseminated, any false advertisement—by United States mails, or in [interstate] commerce by any means, for the purpose of inducing or which is likely to induce, directly or indirectly, the purchase in commerce of food, drugs, devices or cosmetics." Section 55 (a)(1) defines the term

> false advertising as an advertisement other than labeling, which is misleading in a material respect; and in determining whether any advertisement is misleading, there shall be taken into account (among other things) not only representations made or suggested by statement, word or design, device, sound or any combination thereof, but also the extent to which the advertisement fails to reveal facts material in the light of such representations or material with respect to consequences which may result from the use of the commodity. . . .[19]

The FTC now can apply several general principles to aid in determining whether advertising is false or deceptive. "Advertising is misleading if presented in a false context, even though the facts are technically true. Advertising is misleading if it is susceptible to two meanings, one of which is false. Advertising is misleading if expressions of opinion or personal evaluations of intangible qualities are relied upon, which really are subjective claims (although the line between subjective and objective is vague, the tendency is to narrow the area of permissible puffing.)"[20] The FTC need show only that the advertisement in question has the power or tendency to deceive.

CRITICISM OF THE FTC

Certain practices and policies of the FTC have come under heavy criticism in recent years, and some critics question whether the FTC is necessary at all. Richard Posner, for example suggests that adequate market and legal mechanisms may be sufficient. He points out that false claims are not worth making since most consumers know they cannot be true. Consumer sophistication is growing as educational levels rise. Also, because business is dependent upon a reputation for honesty to guarantee repeated sales to the same customer, a policy of deceptive advertising will be costly in the long run. The FTC may not be necessary now, especially, because monopolistic practices are forbidden, and the competition that prevails as a result can place a constraint on false advertising. That is, a competitor can either expose or refute the misinformation carried in an advertisement, or bring suit against the advertiser. In addition, a material misrepresentation in a consumer sale generally will constitute both a breach of contract and a tort. An individual claim may be large enough to justify the cost of a private suit; however, the emergence of the consumer class action suits have provided an incentive for individuals to sue any dishonest advertiser or seller even where an inexpensive item or service is in question.

Posner also notes that "only a small fraction of the FTC's activities in the false advertising area is consistent with a proper allocation of commission resources, considering the character of the false advertising problem and the limitations of the Commission's sanctions. It is possible that the very existence of the Commission serves to deter a great deal of unlawful conduct, but it is unlikely that the FTC's power to deter is very great, given the limitations of its sanctions. Furthermore, against any beneficial deterrent effect must be weighed the cost of enforcement." [22]

Another charge that has been made against the FTC addresses the Commission's practice of changing the interpretation of words and applications of existing rules through complaints issued against individual companies, instead of with formal announcements.

HOSTESS CUPCAKES: COMPLAINT ACTION
BEYOND THE LAW

Continental Baking Company announced through an advertising campaign that it was using a new, more nutritional formula in Hostess Cupcakes. The ensuing FTC complaint alleged deception and unfairness in promoting the nutritional benefit of the product without informing the public that the cupcakes contained 50 percent sugar. There was no precedent for such a complaint, nor any law which required the disclosure of sugar content. The judge in the case found that no advertisements either stated or implied that Hostess Cakes contained all the essential vitamins, and the product did, in fact, contain a higher level of enrichment because of the new formula.

PFIZER UN-BURN: COMPLAINT ACTION FOR DISSEMINATING CORRECT INFORMATION

The FTC asserted in a complaint action that Pfizer did not have "adequate and well controlled scientific studies or tests" to prove assertions made in their advertisements about the ability of UN-BURN to relieve pain. Pfizer argued that there was documented proof of the effectiveness and benefit of ingredients in the product, which were widely recognized in medicine. The hearing examiner dismissed the complaint on the grounds that the company had experience with the ingredients and knowledge of their effectiveness.

The FTC has announced that it will not issue a complaint until the company in question has had an opportunity to present its position and submit written materials; critics contend that the principle should be extended so that all interested and affected parties may respond before a change in the rules is forthcoming. In addition, in 1979, the FTC was warned of Congress' intention to maintain closer scrutiny to guard against "overregulation."

NEW METHODS TO REGULATE ADVERTISING

Litigation remains the most powerful weapon at the disposal of the FTC. However, the FTC is now relying upon more than just cease and desist orders to discourage misleading advertising and is attempting to institute corrective and counter advertising programs as a remedy for deceptive advertising.

Since the cease and desist order cannot compensate consumers who were deceived or any competitor who lost sales, the idea behind corrective advertising is to reduce the benefits to misleading advertisers. In many cases, like Hostess Cupcake, corrective advertising was proposed by the FTC but rejected by the court; however, the remedy has been applied in a number of cases. One was made against Ocean Spray Cranberries, Inc. and its advertising agency, Ted Bates & Company. Ocean Spray signed a consent decree in which it agreed to corrective advertising. To comply with the decree, Ocean Spray had to make certain that one out of every four advertisements of equal time and space, or not less than 25 percent of the medium expenditure (excluding production costs) had to be devoted to corrective advertising for at least one year. The prescribed message read:

> If you've wondered what some of our earlier advertising meant when we said Ocean Spray Cranberry Juice Cocktail has more food energy than orange juice, let us make it clear: we didn't mean vitamins and minerals. Food energy means calories. Nothing more. Food energy is important at breakfast since many of us may not get enough calories, or food energy, to get off to a good start. . . .[23]

While it is hard to disagree with the idea of corrective advertising in concept, the Commission's program has been criticized for discrimination in its selection of cases and inconsistent in its methods of implimentation. Needless to say, the financial burden to business could be astronomical.

COUNTER ADVERTISING

The FTC has proposed that the so-called fairness doctrine be applied to broadcast advertising. This requires that a broadcast station provide individuals the opportunity to present an opposing view when a controversial point of view on a subject of public importance has been aired. The doctrine was first applied in 1968, as a result of Banzhaf v. the FCC,[24] when the FCC indicated that the rule would apply only to cigarette advertising because smoking presented obvious health hazards. However, the courts then extended the fairness doctrine to all commercial advertising in such cases as the Wilderness Society v. NBC, and Retail Store Employees Union, Local 880, v. FCC. Critics maintain that the effectiveness of the doctrine is questionable and compliance with the requirements for air time raises monumental problems for broadcasting facilities. Moreover, counter advertising, by definition in the law, is not commercial speech and under the First Amendment cannot be restrained or controlled as the FTC has proposed.

ADVOCACY ADVERTISING

For many years, many companies have used advocacy advertising to reverse hostile sentiment against them from the public and to gain support for their objectives and interests. One of the most famous campaigns was developed in the thirties for A & P against a tax bill proposed by Congressman Wright Patman. The ads pointed out that the bill would put chain stores out of business, and discussed the stake the public had in the issue. Although the bill had been introduced with one third of the House as co-signers, overwhelming public opposition killed the bill in committee.[25] Then, in the 1950s, a series of articles and studies, such as *The Mass Image of Big Business,* by Gardner and Rainwater, suggested that Americans perceived big business to be too large and remote (which could adversely affect buying decisions). In reaction, numerous companies began advertising campaigns to restore consumer confidence. At the end of the sixties, corporate advertising experienced a renaissance when managers again resorted to advertising to counter anti-business sentiment from environmentalists, consumer groups, and disgruntled employees, as well as from those who maintained that business was accountable for a myriad of social problems such as the oil shortage, inflation, and urban decline.[26] Moreover, the Mobil Oil Company led corporations and trade groups by introducing ads that were more militant.[27] This type of advocacy has continued with ads focused on areas where business feels the press has done an inadequate, or inaccurate, job of covering business news.

While the nature and tone of the ads has changed, dollars spent on advocacy have increased.

In 1971 annual expenditures for corporate image advertising totaled approximately $158 million, by 1976 it was estimated at close to a billion dollars.[28] Several years ago, the Association of National Advertisers found that 30 to 35 percent of corporate advertising was related to the issues of the environment or energy, or explanations of the capitalistic system.[29]

Image advertising attempts to sell ideas rather than products, and it is the use of advertising to accomplish the goals of public relations. As in other types of advertising, there is usually a target audience—employees, the community, government officials, financial analysts, financiers, stockholders, or wholesalers and distributors. There are, however, various sources available to produce the advertisements themselves (advertising departments or agencies usually are not given this responsibility). Sometimes a special in house advertising unit is created, which is directed by top management. The campaign might be assigned to an outside public relations counsel or to a full-service agency which has a corporate advertising unit. The supervision of "controversy advertising" always comes from top management, while public relations departments are regularly responsible for ideas for more general image advertising.[30]

Advocacy advertisements serve two purposes. They are used to improve a company's image or to promote a stand on an issue. The first type is produced in an attempt to improve the overall position of the company in the marketplace by attempting to provide a positive image of the corporation. This image, it is hoped, will influence customers to buy their products. These ads portray the corporation or trade group as a responsible and beneficial entity in society, or might describe the number of jobs provided by the corporation, special community projects it voluntarily supports, or useful products. The ad may seek to identify the products of various divisions with the corporation name. Use of advocacy to project or transfer corporate identity is common when an acquisition has taken place, or when a conglomerate has diversified services and products. Of course, a company may use an image advertising campaign to offset any past or potential negative publicity about the company. A case in point is ITT.

ITT's credibility had been severely damaged by publicity that linked ITT with Chilean politics, as well as with Watergate. Furthermore, surveys showed that less than a quarter of the American people thought the company "cared about" the general public. Only 7 percent thought of it as a leader in technology. Only 34 percent thought its products were reliable. Fewer than half thought it was a very profitable firm. Using the theme, "The best ideas are the ideas that help people," the company engaged in a corporate advertising campaign. As a result, 43 percent of the people began to think ITT cared about the general public, 72 percent regarded it as a leader in technology, and 75 percent felt the firm's products were reliable.[31]

Issue-oriented advertising is noticeably different from advocacy advertising. In this case, advertising is used to present an editorial comment. Sometimes in an "adversorial" an issue will be discussed and the company's point of view will be presented. For example, corporations may use paid advertising to discuss the advantages of the free enterprise system, explain their operations, or refute unfavorable media coverage. More recently the corporations also have been presenting their positions on legislative proposals. Unlike traditional image advertising, advocacy is primarily concerned with public debates and controversial social issues. As a result of this kind of advertising, in April of 1978, the Supreme Court ruled 5 to 4 that corporations were entitled to the protection of the First Amendment, and struck down a Massachusettes law which prohibited corporations from spending money to influence ballot issues that do not materially affect their business. The case, *First National Bank vs. Bellotti,* arose after the bank had spent money to influence a referendum on a personal income tax. The Court ruled that it was unconstitutional to deny them that right. The Supreme Court's decision, however, has not deterred the opposition to the use of advocacy ads. President Carter strongly backed legislation in 1978 designed to limit corporate influence on legislation, supporting those who characterize most corporate advertising as being political in nature and a form of lobbying. The current IRS regulations permit corporations to deduct the cost of advocacy advertising as a business expense provided that it is "ordinary and necessary," is intended to "keep the taxpayer's name before the public," and is "related to the patronage the taxpayer might reasonably expect in the future." At the same time, the law specifically prohibits deductions in connection with lobbying, which is any expenses incurred "in connection with any attempt to influence the general public or segments thereof with respect to legislative matters, elections, or referendums." [32]

Mobil Oil has developed a systematic approach to classifying institutional advertising, which may be useful to others employing image advertising. The company has four categories for its corporate advertising, and determines the tax status accordingly. Group 1 consists of ads of the so-called "Red Cross" variety, urging viewers to watch Mobil-sponsored programs on public (educational) television networks, support local opera and theater, and donate to worthy causes. Group 2 deals with fuel conservation and safe driving, noncontroversial ads about subjects on which the company felt that it had some expertise and whose issues were considered to be in the public interest. Group 3 deals with issues of a broad socioeconomic nature, such as technology and conservation. Group 4 advertisements are in the nondeductible category. This approach also involves submitting all ads to an outside counsel for an opinion on deductibility.

EVALUATION AND EFFECTS

Unlike a product advertising campaign, it may be difficult to determine whether an advocacy or image advertising camapign is reaching the intended audiences, spreading the message of the corporation, and effective in altering public opinion. "Advocacy" as William R. Dill, former Dean of the Graduate School of Business Administration at New York University pointed out, "may be preaching to the already converted." Secondly, advocacy may attempt to cure a symptom, rather than a cause of an attitude business may want to change. Thirdly, business must be careful of "backlash," especially in using controversy adversorials where the value of the campaign may be completely undetermined.

Donald W. Jugenheimer of the William White School of Journalism at the University of Kansas points out; "Companies want to improve their 'images' through the use of advertising, but when the advertisements have run, nobody seems to know if the 'image' was improved or not." Jugenheimer responds with a plan for evaluation: (1) Avoid using the concept of "image" and promote an issue that can be evaluated. (2) Develop specific, achievable objectives for each advertisement. (3) To do this, plan in advance a survey to determine the attitude of the public beforehand and then another survey afterwards to see if the public has been swayed.

A COMPANY CALLED TRW

An image advertising campaign was undertaken by TRW, Inc., which spent $2.5 million dollars on such ads in 1978. The ads ran in business magazines that reach investors and professional investment counselors, a definable audience. However, ads also appeared on news programs, the "Today Show," and during sports and artistic presentations on television. The object of the campaign ostensibly was to reach the general public and inform them of the diversity of TRW's product line and the range of the corporation as a whole. Moreover, TRW is *not unionized,* would like to remain that way and wanted to enhance their employees' image of the company. The company also wanted to influence regulators and legislators to be favorably disposed towards the company because of its Credit Reporting Division, which is the largest operation of its kind in the country and an important part of TRW's business. Because rights of privacy issues are involved in gathering credit facts and information about unpaid bills, regulation in the industry is high, and there is a potential for even more regulation in the future.

The image advertising campaign, a sharp departure from the company's tradition of inexpensive print advertising in trade journals, was undertaken following a 1974 study which showed that TRW had an *identity void:* there was a lack of public awareness about the company. After five years, results showed that in Washington, D.C., one of ten major target markets, nine out of ten people with average incomes of $30,000 were aware of TRW, and two-thirds rated the company's reputation as good or excellent.

PART II

CHAPTER 8

Disclosure and Compliance

Nearly 5000 different federal forms must be filled out by business corporations and executives. The time it takes to complete this task is estimated to be more than 150 million hours per year. The total cost of both disclosure and regulatory compliance by companies and direct expenses of government regulation exceeds $100 billion a year.[1] General Motors estimates that for a single year the documents that it must file in connection with the certification of its cars make a stack 15 stories high. Dow Chemical estimated that in 1975 government regulation cost the company $147 million and that $50 million of that was "excessive"—costs beyond those required by good business practices.[2] It should therefore come as no surprise that the deflection of private investment from productive uses to disclosure and regulation has meant the loss of potential growth for the economy as a whole. One fourth of the nation's potential annual increase in productivity has been lost, according to Edward Denison of the Brookings Institute, as a result of these direct and hidden costs of disclosure and regulation.[3]

Perhaps as a result of this fact, President Carter stated as one of his key campaign objectives reducing what he called "nonproductive" intervention and increasing "useful" intervention in an attack on "the mess in Washington." Regulatory reform has, therefore, passed beyond being a worthwhile goal to become something of a political necessity.[4]

The expense of disclosure is obviously not entirely useless, however. Clean air and water, safe products and working conditions, and fairer stock and commodity markets are worth a good deal, and many economists try to ascribe a real dollar figure to all the benefits of disclosure and regulation. That is, despite the outcries from business that these horrendous costs are unnecessary, government administrators respond that failures in the ordinary market system of business brought about the need for controls and oversight agencies. Stock frauds, misleading financial

73

reports, unsafe products, polluted air and water, and dangerous working conditions were the result of business practices that made regulation a necessity. Business managers retort that rampaging bureaucracy is the reason for intervention, not "market failures" or "inadequacies of the free enterprise system" (euphemisms of economic analysis for the problems of diseconomies of scale).

The business sector has become increasingly vociferous in its attack on overregulation and overdisclosure. Said Paul Oreffice, President of Dow Chemical USA, "overregulation is the biggest single danger to being viable as a business." A.R. Marusi, Chairman and Chief Executive of Borden, used even stronger language: "Things have gone too far, and the evidence is all around us." "Wave" . . . "tide" . . . "jungle" . . . "plague," are the words journalists and business executives use to describe requirements of the government in controlling business activity. Even top officials in the regulatory field agree. John Shenefield, former assistant attorney general in charge of the antitrust division, contends there is "a serious possibility that public restraints through regulation will, in the long-run, pose a threat to competition and consumer interest in the energy industries at least as important as private anticompetitive behavior."

Concluding a three-year study, a blue ribbon commission of the American Bar Association criticized disclosure in regulatory agencies as inefficient, inflexible and full of wasteful bureaucratic complications. According to a 1978 study of American Opinion sponsored by *U.S. News and World Report,* less than 7 percent rated regulatory agencies as "good or better" in their "ability to get things done" and 81 percent agreed that "competition is better than government regulation to make sure that public gets what it pays for." (Despite this assessment, 46 percent of all households surveyed agreed that "the cost to the taxpayers of regulating business is well worth it.")

During the past half century Congress has tended to create an agency to handle any problem that arose, with no coordination or overall planning among agencies. The result is that many regulatory agencies operate autonomously, are uniquely structured, and may have overlapping jurisdiction with other agencies.[5]

DISCLOSURE REGULATION: A BRIEF BACKGROUND

Whatever the reasons for the comparatively recent system of massive intervention, almost no one disputes that decisions of managers are today influenced and, in some cases, controlled by regulatory policy, procedure, and oversight. In certain industries, government regulators determine profit percentages, prices, marketing regions, method of financing, and even lines of business. The government directly and fully regulates such important industries as broadcast media, transportation, telephone and mail service, and gas and electricity—the so-called "natural monopolies." While society tends to view intervention as a new phenomenon, regulatory law has ancient roots, predating the American capitalist system by at least 4000 years. Regulatory law first was established in Hammurabi's Codes in the eighteenth century B.C. when the Babylonian king established building code regulations which made the builder responsible if a structure collapsed and killed someone.

Monarchs of Tudor England imposed wage and price controls, and, like their counterparts in Europe, granted monopolies to certain trades as political favors. Virtually all major industries at that time, from shipping and importing to button and saddle manufacturing, were dominated by monopolies. More than 700 monopolies controlled commerce and industry in Britain. The same was true in France and the rest of Europe. Indeed, for most of the history of commerce as we know it, regulation has been a pervasive element in the climate of business. Over the centuries, control of business and the "media" by kings, emperors, magistrates, and officials was taken for granted in most of Europe, Asia, Latin America, and the Middle East.

BUSINESS AND MEDIA FREEDOM: AN HISTORICAL PARALLEL

The concept that business and the press have the rights of free enterprise and free speech is uniquely the product of a Western European heritage, and is distinctly modern. Although during the brief golden ages of the ancient Athenian democracy and Roman Republic the individual's right to engage in commerce and free speech were respected, these periods were the exception in the 2000-year history of Western civilization.

Not until 1215, when King John of England was forced to sign the Magna Carta, were common people awarded certain basic rights. Popular protest in the British Isles and the increasing power of the common man finally lead in England to passage of the Statute of Monopolies (1623-1634) which eliminated many monopolies except in new manufacturing and in the rights of the inventor of a product. The movement for a free enterprise system spread to America and to France in the eighteenth century and was an important factor in their revolutions.

The colonists in America had long protested the colonial companies, which were the exceptions to the antimonopoly rulings. Colonists were prohibited from engaging in commerce outside of the British Empire and were required to trade and sell raw materials and buy finished goods exclusively from the English companies. Resentment against these restrictions, coupled with development of autonomous industries and severe taxes, intensified and triggered a rebellion. In the Declaration of Independence, Jefferson accused King George III of erecting "a multitude of new offices to harass our people and eat out their substance."

Thus the American political experiment was also an experiment founded upon radical principles of political, commercial, and journalistic freedom. Political rights sanctioned and enforced by law paralleled individual, commercial, and journalistic rights of free speech. Men became free to vote, to enter business, and to print their views. That original concept of freedom written into the Constitution and Bill of Rights provided the business environment for America's first 150 years: laissez-faire.

If we take pride in many of these traditions as rightfully American, it is nonetheless necessary to realize that most of our basic legal concepts relevant to business enterprise have been derived from the common law of England: protection against public disorder, protection against arbitrary seizure of property, access to impartial courts for the settlement of disputes, and, most importantly, freedom of contracts.[6] The only significant restraint upon these freedoms resulted from state and local blue laws restricting business hours at certain times in deference to religious observance.

CHAPTER 9

Administrative Agencies

Although the system of business regulation in the United States was developed slowly throughout the first 150 years, today administrative and regulatory agencies are found at all levels of government. They perform an enormous range of functions and are so varied in size and structure that no single definition or description is applicable. At the federal level, there are over 100 agencies, but the discussion here will focus on agencies which are of general concern to many companies and industries. These agencies were created by Congress, sometimes at the behest of the President. The most powerful and well-known ones are independent, while the others are under the control of the Executive Branch. Thus, the Interstate Commerce Commission (ICC), Federal Trade Commission (FTC), and the Securities and Exchange Commission (SEC), for example, were created by Congress and are independent of the executive branch. Other agencies, considered part of the executive branch, are The Food and Drug Administration (FDA), which is part of the Health and Welfare Department, and the Mining Enforcement and Safety Administration, which is part of the Interior Department. Theoretically, the only direct control the President has over the agencies that are part of the executive branch is the power to appoint commissioners and administrators, with the approval of the Senate, and to control their funds, through the Office of Management and Budget. Since the terms of office for the independent commissioners may run longer than presidential terms—seven years is typical—the only real influence the President may have is through moral suasion. The President can and often does use this influence, but may also use the news media to initiate action through public comment.

Our system of government is founded on a strong belief in the separation of powers of the executive, legislative and judicial branches. Many regulatory agencies assume all these functions. Legal and philosophical questions arise about whether an agency should, for example, be able to investigate, prosecute and judge a complaint initiated by the agency itself, or whether this might be an illegal conjoining of powers. One of the complaints raised against regulation is that the agencies are largely unchecked in the use of all three powers.

GROWTH OF BUSINESS REGULATION

In 1824 the Army Corps of Engineers became the river dredgers, and dam and bridge builders of America, and in effect the first regulatory agency. Created by government to solve an economic and social problem, the Corps of Engineers was not set up to regulate any segment or business; rather it superceded the role of private enterprise.

Direct regulation of business began in the eighteenth century, but regulation was first greatly extended during the trust-busting period from 1890 to 1915 when the Sherman and Clayton Antitrust Acts were passed and the Federal Trade Commission was created. Then, during the New Deal era, dozens of agencies were established to take over management of whole areas of the economy and business. During the period of the sixties and seventies, even more agencies have been formed in response to environmental, energy, and economic problems.

The expiration of the charter of the Second Bank of the United States in 1836, the bank panic of 1837, and finally, the general pressure on currency caused by the Civil War gave rise to the Banking Act of 1863. Under this act, the Comptroller of the Currency was given the power to charter and regulate national banks and to require disclosure. The Comptroller's office thereby became the first federal government body to require disclosure from business entities.

As the American transportation industry expanded, with the growth of shipping, toll roads, canals, and, especially, railroads, unfair trade practices became sufficiently blatant and widespread that once again intervention was required to correct abuses. Congress reacted by passing the Interstate Commerce Act of 1887 which created the first independent regulatory agency. The power of the ICC was extended from the railroads to all forms of commerce and upheld by a ruling of the Supreme Court. The Court justified expansion of federal authority through the "commerce clause" in the Constitution. (Article I, Section 8, granted Congress the power to "regulate Commerce with foreign Nationals, and among the several States, and with the Indian Tribes." Regulatory activity of Congress has been supported by the courts under a broad interpretation of this clause.) Today, the commerce clause remains the primary legal basis for federal disclosure and regulatory law.

From the 1880s, the dramatic growth of the trust cartels and "robber baron" fortunes inevitably changed the economic structure of the economy, causing consolidation of power and wealth. Not only in railroads, but in almost every major industry of that time, these vertically and horizontally integrated conglomerates dominated each market they entered. As well as featuring the creation of the predecessors of the modern corporation, this period witnessed the spawning of substantial public distrust of big business and powerful institutions.

The Sherman Antitrust Act was introduced to deal with such giants as Standard Oil, and the infamous whiskey, sugar, lead, and cotton oil trusts. Enforcement of the Sherman Act became the responsibility of the Justice Department's antitrust division, headed by an assistant attorney general. Antitrust activities may be enforced through the court system in one of two ways. The Justice Department may enforce laws and private suits by individuals may be brought to seek compensation for injuries suffered as a result of a violation of an antitrust law.

Unfortunately, the Act, which was instituted to make monopolistic contracts or conspiracies to monopolize trade illegal, did not succeed in curbing such activities for the first ten years after it was passed. This failure occured partly because the federal courts, even the Supreme Court, failed to enforce the Act's provisions and interpret its broad language to curtail abuses. Instead, corporations were under the law granted the status of individuals and were granted the right to make deals, fix prices, and form monopolies under the rights of free speech and commerce. Therefore, although President Theodore Roosevelt was pictured in cartoons as a trust buster, the cartels were, in fact, stronger when Roosevelt left office in 1908 than when he took office in 1900.

To put teeth into the Sherman Act, Congress passed the Clayton Act, which made it illegal to create an incipient monopoly. Section 7 of the Act, as amended in 1950 by the Celler-Kefauver Act, prohibits corporate acquisitions which might result in the creation of a monopoly or might substantially lessen competition. However, of even greater importance, in many ways, than passage of the Clayton Act of 1914, was the creation that same year of the Federal Trade Commission to monitor all pricing and potentially anticompetitive behavior on the part of companies. As part of its policing activities, the FTC was given the power to exact periodic and virtually continuous disclosure of business practices.

Another important step by Congress in the period between passage of the Sherman and Clayton Acts was the creation of the Federal Reserve System. In effect, the 12 regional Federal Banks became the "bankers' bank" providing specific services such as selling rediscount commercial paper on which the member banks make loans, issuing notes or paper currency, such as Federal Reserve Notes, clearing and collecting funds, acting as a depository for reserve funds, and acting as a fiscal agent and depository for the government.[1] Members are regulated, and disclosure requirements are extensive.

Even though regulatory agencies had been established, disclosure requirements were quite limited prior to the Depression of the 1930s. Business managers were able to work without major interference from the government—or the public. As long as the economy was performing well, there was little pressure on the government to meddle in the affairs of the private sector. However, after the stock market crashed in 1929, banks and business soon began to fail. Many believed their hardships were caused by business institutions and the fundamental change which had occurred in the free enterprise system. Confidence in business and industry deteriorated, and then evaporated, creating a clamor for economic planning and leadership from the federal government. As a result, in 1930, the Federal Power Act established the Federal Power Commission, now part of the Federal Energy Regulatory Commission, to regulate interstate transportation of fuel, the wholesale price of electricity and natural gas, and the routes of natural gas pipelines. Publication of *The Jungle,* by Upton Sinclair, had led to passage of the Pure Food and Drug Act in 1906, but to assure the safety and effectiveness of drugs, the pureness of foods, and proper labeling, the Food and Drug Administration was established in 1931.

Franklin Roosevelt responded to the economic breakdown with the New Deal and more regulatory agencies, like the FDIC, SEC, FCC, and CAB.[2] As a result, business began to lose its position of autonomy as the government began to regulate it. Because the FTC had a record for strict enforcement, the Commission was used as a model for the new agencies. All the quasilegislative and quasijudicial powers of the FTC, such as the power to investigate, prosecute, hold hearings and trials, set rules and impose fines, were incorporated into the new agencies. This period is of fundamental importance because the powers granted to the agencies became accepted as part of the government's regulatory function.

Two important agencies were established in 1934. Responsibility for regulation of communications, formerly under the ICC and the Federal Radio Commission, was transferred to a single commission, the Federal Communications Commission. The FCC controls telephone and telegraph rates and lines, licenses interstate broadcasting, sets the standards for qualification of station operators, and maintains the ethics of the airwaves. In addition, the FCC is responsible for enforcing the fairness doctrine.

The other agency, the Securities and Exchange Commission, is perhaps the most important of all in a discussion of disclosure. In 1933, Congress, as result of the 1929 crash and dishonesty in securities transactions, was confronted with the problem of regulating corporate stock and offerings of securities.

THE SECURITIES AND EXCHANGE COMMISSION

At the time that Congress confronted these problems, there were two dominant viewpoints expressed concerning the means for dealing with stock offerings. One view favored government screening of all securities offered to the public. As conceived in the Thompson Bill, the federal government would have the right to prevent the sale of any company's securities if they involved a high risk. This view was called "blue sky," since it was patterned after state legislation aimed at preventing swindlers from selling stock in nothing more than the blue sky.

Opposing regulations through the Thompson Bill were advocates of "disclosure" as the method for most effectively regulating the securities markets. They opposed making specific judgments as to the value and risk of specific securities. Instead, they favored enactment of legislation to ensure access to information. Determination of what should be disclosed would rest on what information would be necessary to make a prudent investment. Disclosure would also serve to regulate any questionable activities in the securities industry and markets. As a champion of disclosure, Justice Brandeis compared disclosure for corporation securities to the pure food legislation, which did not require manufacturers to state the relative value of their products, but gave the public the ability to make their own decisions based on the disclosure of contents.

President Roosevelt called for legislation to create "better supervision of purchase and sale in the exchange . . . with least possible interference to honest business." He rejected blue sky legislation and proposals for radical intervention in the markets. He told Congress:

The federal government cannot and should not take any action which might be construed as approving or guaranteeing that newly issued securities are sound in the sense that their value will be maintained or that the properties that they represent will earn profit. There is, however, an obligation upon us to insist that every issue of new securities to be sold in interstate commerce should be accompanied by publicity and information. . . . This proposal adds to the ancient rule of *caveat emptor* [let the buyer beware] the further doctrine let the seller also beware. It puts the burden of telling the whole truth on the seller. It would give impetus to honest dealing in securities and thereby bring back public confidence.

The logic behind the policy of disclosure was that if a corporation wanted to sell securities in the interstate market, the federal government would grant a license on the condition that the company disclose its affairs. Thus, the Securities Act of 1933 called for registering all securities prior to their sale and for supplying each potential investor with a prospectus, which was required to contain financial and other information necessary for an intelligent investment decision. The Act also established criminal liability for fraud in sale of securities which were improperly registered. Fraud could be claimed if the registration contained false or misleading information or omitted relevent information. The underwriter, accountant, any appraiser participating in preparation of the registration, the directors or any person named in the registration as a future director, and the signers of the registration papers would be held liable.

In 1934, by an amendment to the Securities Exchange Act, the scope of disclosure was broadened to include secondary markets, or stock exchanges where trading took place. (Under the 1933 Act only the primary or the original offering had been effected.) The Securities and Exchange Commission also was created. A corporation had to file with both an exchange and the SEC before its stock could be publicly traded.

The Securities Exchange Act, as amended in 1934, brought dealers and traders under tight government control by requiring them to record all their transactions in detail and to file reports each year with the SEC. Rule 10b 5 extended liability for fraud to brokers and dealers who used the mail to deceive investors; this rule also provided for the prosecution of anyone attempting to manipulate a market. Under this rule, an insider, defined as any director or officer of a corporation or as any person who owned at least 10 percent of a stock were required to file a separate statement with the SEC indicating the number of shares held in the company and to inform the SEC of any purchase or sale within ten days after the end of the month in which the transaction occurs.[3] This disclosure requirement has come to represent one of the most radical extensions of disclosure under the Act. Insiders now includes anyone and everyone with any knowledge of special circumstances that might cause movement in the price of a stock. Anyone who receives such information and acts on it can be prosecuted and imprisoned.

Enforcement has traditionally been the SEC's main responsibility. And, as a result, in fiscal 1977, for example, the division instituted 166 civil suits versus 56 a decade earlier.[4] Given the workload, the Commission could not possibly go to court with every case, and some 90 percent of the civil lawsuits are closed through negotiated consent orders. The reason most companies agree to such orders, most critics say, is to get the SEC off their backs. Seldom do consent orders stop ongoing violations. In addition, because the SEC prolongs investigations for years in some cases, it is argued that any ensuing litigation is irrelevant. Yet, the cost and time that companies have already spent in making full disclosure and conferring with lawyers constitutes a de facto penalty without due process.

The theory of disclosure in exchange for a license was drastically changed in 1964, by a comparatively little-known amendment to the Exchange Act. This required all corporations with 500 or more stockholders and $1 million or more worth of assets, whether they wanted anything from the government or not, to make periodic filings. Since that time, the SEC has been working toward a policy of continuous disclosure, which was described by former SEC chairman Ray Garrett:

> The Commission has, over the last few years, been carrying out a program of integration of the disclosure requirements of the Securities Act of 1933, which is aimed basically at public offerings, with those of the Securities Act of 1934, which is more directly related to trading activities. The object of this program is to create a system of continuous disclosure, so that any investor, at any time, has access to the most recent information about most publicly held corporations. The person making an investment decision does not care whether the securities are coming directly from the corporations, as part of an offering, or are coming from another stockholder, through the trading markets. In either case, the investor wants and should have access to the same type of information.[5]

In 1969 the SEC issued new requirements for reporting line of business information in registration statements for companies wishing to issue new stock. These requirements were extended in 1970 to annual reports filed with the SEC on Form 10-K; and, in October 1974, they were further extended to the annual reports to security holders of companies filing with the SEC. The New York Stock Exchange issued a "White Paper" in 1973 urging line of business information in annual reports, at least as extensive as that required in the 10-K.

The SEC and the Financial Accounting Standards Board ruled that segmented information had to be reported in the financial statements of a diversified corporation or group. Otherwise, information about operations of any particular segment would be unavailable if only the combined figures of a conglomerate or highly diversified company were presented. The arguments were made that one company must disclose figures for any segment representing 10 percent or more of its business, while a competitor in the same line of business might not have to disclose such information because it represented less than 10 percent of the business. That argument failed, and all publicly traded corporations must now disclose profits and margins for any division or product representing more than 10 percent of its total business.

The requirement by the SEC that corporations submit economic projections and other "soft information" in SEC filings has been under study by the SEC and by independent analysts for some years. It presents to publicly held companies and the securities industry the most complex and most difficult questions imaginable. The long-term objectives are laudable and are supported by many observers and participants in business, media, law, and regulatory bodies. They feel that the projections can result in more realistic and more meaningful disclosure by business of its actual and future condition. It is believed that this disclosure will help the public, potential investors, professional advisors, and the government. Nevertheless, there remains widespread opposition among corporate management and accountants who fear that the SEC's definition of projections is so broad that anything management might say regarding projections would expose them legally to charges of inaccuracy or fraud. However, the critics fail to take into account that some companies were giving out unsubstantiated forecasts and projections designed to enhance the company image.

The SEC, in a recent court case, won the right to require that even more information be disclosed in tender offers. First, post acquisition steps planned by an acquiring company following a successful tender offer must be disclosed. Second, the public must be informed of valuations by the offerer and other outsiders. Third, the personal self-interest of different participants in tender offers should be clearly revealed because, in the past, far too many deals were made "under the table" and the details never were revealed to unsuspecting stockholders or professional advisors, much less to government regulators. In 1975 fixed brokerage commissions were abolished by the SEC. The Consolidated Tape System was also started so that bid-and-asked differentials for securities traded on major exchanges across the country would be presented on one screen. In June 1975, President Ford signed the Securities Acts Amendments, which granted the SEC power to implement the National Market System which would consolidate all the different securities markets. The NMS would give investors the opportunity to select a bid or asked price from anywhere and, in effect, eliminate the multiple market system.

In October 1977, the SEC froze listings of new stock options and announced an in-depth investigation of the industry. This move occurred just four years after the SEC had allowed the Chicago Board of Options Exchange to open and two years after it allowed options trading on the American Stock Exchange. Two years later the SEC recommended that the moratorium on new listings be extended, effectively curtailing the growth of options as an investment vehicle. In December of 1977, President Ford signed the Foreign Corrupt Practices Act to empower the SEC to prevent corporate bribery and other illegal behavior. This law was designed to force companies not only to cease illegal foreign payments but also to disclose all such current and past improper activities.

In January 1978, SEC Chairman Harold Williams proposed that all corporate directors be independent of management and that boards should have independent audit committees. He proposed that firms should indicate the status of directors and structure of their boards in their reports to stockholders on the presumption that requiring such disclosure would encourage companies to structure their boards accordingly. The business community became especially upset over the SEC's proposal to label each director as "management," "affiliated non-management," or "independent." Such "forced classification," says Paul J. Mason, chief counsel for the American Council of Life Insurance, "gives the impression that some people are tainted; classifying them will cut off a good part of the supply of potential directors." [6] Many argue, as does John C. Whitehead, partner of Goldman Sachs, that Williams' ideal board could result in the government's appointing directors. The SEC and other critics of management say that these new measures are necessary because most boards are beholden to management. Thus, the SEC began to ask for more information on such things as the remuneration of all corporate executives, including personal loans, house mortgage arrangements, holidays, trips, cars, houses, gifts, and more than 30 other items. (Even before 1978, the SEC had required from each candidate their business history and a list of other directorships held.)

The most significant of new SEC proposals is that all corporations be federally chartered instead of being chartered by separate states, some of which are regarded as too lenient in their oversight. The classic example of a lenient state is Delaware, where many American corporations are registered. Some corporations, especially in shipping, register under foreign "flags of convenience"—such as those of Liberia or Panama—to avoid taxes, reporting and disclosure requirements, and labor unions. State governments and many corporate representatives are opposed to any move the SEC will make to require federal chartering.

The SEC concluded over the years that it has a responsibility to help the general public understand how corporations should function, although it has required such sophisticated disclosure that the general public cannot possibly understand the information reported. This endeavor, however, may be necessary:

> . . . because the present stockholders owe their wealth to the ability to pass it on to somebody else via a public market, and future stockholders may be interested in acquiring that stock because of required disclosures for public companies, it is entirely reasonable to require disclosure of financial affairs. . . .[7]

Yet in the view of many critics the SEC's use of disclosure as a means of forcing business change and practice is an extremely questionable use of the disclosure principle.

The Securities and Exchange Commission is under attack for seven practices, according to a *Business Week* survey. It uses publicity to punish a firm or individual when it does not have sufficient facts to justify formal charges. The SEC frequently alters its policies by ad hoc decisions, thus changing rules retroactively. It has written new rules on disclosure which touch areas beyond its jurisdiction, especially by thrusting itself into the internal operations of corporations. It has become involved with controlling accounting practices and has adopted unrealistic interpretations of the profession's rules. Its enforcement division, which built up an impressive record in bringing corporate bribery to light, has become overzealous, and has undermined its supposed objectivity. The SEC has been accused of letting offenders off without punishment or with little more than a slap on the wrist. It has attempted to design a fundamental restructuring of the nation's securities markets, though Congress mandates it only to facilitate implementation of those changes.[8]

THE FEDERAL TRADE COMMISSION

Several agencies have to require disclosure reports from corporations to all agencies simultaneously. The SEC for example, resisted an effort by the Federal Trade Commission to gain access to this information and to have the SEC require the information in such form as the Federal Trade Commission could use for antitrust purposes. The SEC, over the protest of the Federal Trade Commission, refused on the basis that such disclosure was for securities investment purposes and not for enforcing antitrust laws. The FTC finally went to Congress to get authorization to expand their disclosure requirements, which they did in 1974.

The Federal Trade Commission requires that large manufacturing companies report detailed financial information for each line of business. The corporations have resisted this bitterly on the grounds that the FTC is simply demanding more information than they can reasonably be expected to furnish. However, in November of 1978, both American Cynamid Company and Deering Millikin, Inc. lost appeals in the U.S. Court of Appeals, and all businesses must now supply the information should the FTC require it.

The Federal Trade Commission first had required that companies submit to the government full documentation of sales and cost of goods sold. It has since demanded to see copies of marketing strategy as well. Often, such strategies have been developed with investments of billions of dollars in order to establish and protect a competitive position in a highly competitive marketplace. Because the information, which outlines past, present, and future marketing strategies might fall into the hands of another marketing company and severely erode a company's position, several major firms have gone to court the defy the FTC. They refused to turn over sensitive marketing strategies on the basis that the FTC is incapable of giving them the protection that they have a right to demand.

Corporations, quite naturally see great risk in divulging such data. A confidential memo can be shuffled into the wrong agency pigeon hole deliberately or accidentally. Under the Freedom of Information Act, competitors can file a request and, under certain circumstances, receive legitimate trade secrets—for free.

SOCIAL ISSUES

In the sixties, public concern focused on social issues, and the Office of Contract Compliance was created in 1962 and administered by the Labor Department. It was responsible for prohibiting racial and sexual discrimination by employers with federal contracts. In 1962, the Equal Employment Opportunity Commission was formed to investigate and conciliate complaints of employment discrimination based on race, religion, and sex. While the EEOC is criticized for lack of real clout, the commission has won some major court cases.

By the end of the sixties, social concern arose over environmental and consumer protection. In 1970, the National Highway Safety Administration began regulating manufacturers of cars, trucks, buses, motorcycles, trailers, and tires. The agency also set safety standards. The Environmental Protection Agency was also established in 1970. With a budget approaching $1 billion, the EPA develops standards for restricting the pollution of the air and water, and for limiting noise, pesticides, radiation, and toxic substances. The agency conducts monitoring and surveillance programs, and provides technical and financial assistance to state and local governments.

The Occupational Safety and Health Administration was created by Congress in 1971 as part of the Labor Department, to establish and enforce specific standards and recordkeeping requirements concerning the work environment and the health of the workers. Then, Congress established the Consumer Product Safety Commission in 1972 to ensure the quality of all consumer products. The breadth of the law is apparent from its definition of a consumer product. The term includes any articles produced or distributed for sale to, or use by, a consumer in or around a permanent or temporary household or residence, a school, in recreation, or other use.[9]

In response to a sudden and potentially dangerous situation, the OPEC (Organization of Petroleum Exporting Countries) oil embargo of 1973 to 1974, the Congress created the Federal Energy Administration. Later, the FEA was incorporated into the Department of Energy. Virtually everything and anything to do with energy falls under the jurisdiction of the DOE, including pricing, allocation of product, research, and policy formulation.

In 1974, the Commodity Futures Trading Act and the Employee Retirement Income Security Act (ERISA) were enacted. The Commodities Futures Trading Commission regulates trading on ten commodities exchanges and regulates brokers and dealers. Through pension welfare programs, the Labor Department enforces the provisions of ERISA. The agency oversees the 1.8 million pension and benefit plans governed by the Act.

CORPORATE CHALLENGE TO DISCLOSURE DECREES

From the beginning of disclosure requirements imposed in the 1930s, corporations challenged the federal government on whether business should be required to disclose earnings to permit the public, including their competitors, know their position. In a famous case of the thirties involving the American Sumatra Tobacco Company, the courts held that the SEC could reasonably deny confidential treatment to the required filings on sales, cost of goods sold, and gross profit. The information had to be provided, even though it might reveal something to a competitor, because the availability of the data is in the public interest. Forty years later, this remains the rationale for all disclosure.

The question of degree of disclosure required by regulators is up to the "good sense" of an agency. Yet, if any federal agency fails to show good sense, there is very little that the courts can do. This particular problem is well illustrated in a government case brought against Arthur Young and Company (one of the major accounting firms) when it resisted an SEC subpoena. Arthur Young had been the auditor for a company, SCA Services in Boston, which was involved in alleged fraud and misappropriation of funds by its officers. The SEC subpoenaed from Arthur Young 2000 correspondence folders and 200 other folders; a total of 275 linear feet of paper. The accountants resisted on the grounds that providing the information would disrupt their operations, since papers were scattered throughout 15 offices. They could not do their own work if they lent the papers to the Commission, and to make photostatic copies of all the material would cost over $100,000. The dragnet subpoena was unfair and unjust, but the court said, in effect, it could not overrule the judgment of an agency as to what it needs to conduct its work, as long as the request is within reasonable bounds. The court enforced the subpoena subject only to the question of whether the SEC might have to reimburse Arthur Young for the $100,000 if the cost turned out to be that much. The key question today is not just the quantity of disclosure forced by government agencies but its quality, that is, whether the information that is being demanded from companies is necessary to protecting the public.

The Arthur Young case shows that there is nothing the courts can do when an agency is making unsound judgments short of outlandish pressure.

To resist what they consider unreasonable or improper agency demands for data, businesses are "flexing new legal muscles and going to court to block, undercut or at the very least modify the inspection and investigative procedure of a number of government agencies—often even before the businesses are accused of any wrongdoing." [10]

Part of the reason for businesses' more militant attitude is that the courts have become more sensitive to complaints about the procedures used by regulators. The courts' position rests on a U.S. Supreme Court decision in May of 1978 in the case of a plumber, F.G. Barlow, who argued that he had the right to throw OSHA inspectors out of his plumbing and heating shop because they did not have a warrant. The case is being cited as a landmark for business rights.

When the Environmental Protection Agency sent a team of engineers to a Dow Chemical Company Plant in Midland, Michigan, to photograph a coal-fired plant at the huge chemical complex, the company refused to admit them. Instead of trying to get a warrant, which Dow would have challenged in court, the EPA chartered a plane and took photographs of the entire Dow complex. The photographer took about 100 pictures with a special mapping camera. Dow sued, alleging invasion of privacy, unreasonable search, and denial of due process. Dow won an injunction impounding the pictures until the case is settled.

General Motors, two of its dealers, Chrysler Corporation, and American Motors Corporation recently sued the Federal Trade Commission to halt a two-year, wide-range study of the economic performance of the auto industry, arguing that it was in violation of the Fourth Amendment because it is "unfocused" and is being conducted "by seizing and sifting through confidential and proprietary information . . . on the mere possibility that some unknown and unsuspected law violation might be detected."

COUNTERING THE REGULATORY AGENCIES

Controlling government agencies that are going beyond what the law has mandated is difficult because the law is very general and its interpretation is left up to the regulators. Many regulators cling to the mistaken notion that collecting information will solve problems. As a result, government warehouses bulge with data and papers collected from companies in the belief that somewhere within them lies the answers. No one will ever know.

Even small businesses are forced to spend from $15 to $20 billion in completing government paperwork. Some chief executives estimate that dealing with government takes up 25 percent to 50 percent of their time, which drastically reduces the time they can spend on actually running their companies.[11] Partly to overcome this problem, General Motors, for example, details 22,300 employees to federal paperwork.[12]

RESULT: AN UNCONTROLLABLE INCREASE IN OVERHEAD

To the cost of collecting and filing disclosure documents must be added the cost of employing legal counsel to advise on what, when, how, and to whom, and whether to disclose. The cost of government fines, civil damage suits, the private suits that sometimes accompany governments' civil suits, and a portion of increasing expenses for lobbying and advocacy advertising expenses are attributable to regulatory activity. In sum, for every major U.S. corporation, all of the regulation has meant an enormous increase in overhead expense.

The cost of social legislation has affected industry in other ways. Thus, the lead industries association recently estimated that 80 percent of American lead smelting and refining palnts will be unable to meet the EPA's strict new air standards and will have to close, as have dozens of foundries and older steel plants. Whereas giants like General Motors or Ford can afford the cost of adding pollution control equipment to their cars and modernizing factories; Chrysler and American Motors cannot. The effect is that as Chrysler and American Motors become even more marginal, and lose more of their share of the market, General Motors and Ford become larger, and the market for automobiles thereby becomes less competitive.

Wellesley College economist Carolyn Shaw Bell estimates that the cost of consumer products has increased because companies have passed along the cost of regulation. In this way, the costs of regulation have added at least three-quarters of a point to the nation's inflation rate.[13] The following examples dramatize these inflationary pressures. Steel has been pushed up in price at least $8 a ton by antipollution environmental protection laws (and, as a result, American steel has become less competitive on the world market). In the largest industry in this country, construction, it is estimated that building code and materials regulations add $1500 to $2500 to the cost of a house. For automobiles, the extra cost is estimated to be at least $600 per car.[14] Of course, these higher prices lead to a demand for inflationary wage increases to keep pace with rising costs, and caused productivity to fall from 3 percent to 1 percent since the sixties.[15] Even the President's Council on Wage and Price Stability admits: "there can be no doubt that much of the productivity collapse in mining and utilities can be attributed to social legislation that protects the environment and safety of miners." [16]

The costs of complying with the requirements of agencies that enforce social legislation constitute a major portion of the $100 billion that American business and industry spend on compliance with all regulatory rulings and requirements. Among the more prominent of these agencies are the Environmental Protection Agency, the Consumer Product Safety Commission, the Department of Energy, and the Occupational Safety and Health Administration. Approximately 92 percent of total federal regulatory expenditures and 39 percent of the compliance expense of business can be attributed to these four agencies[17]

Various analysts see several crucial differences between these newer agencies and their forebears. For example, economist Murray Weidenbaum, head of the Center for the Study of American Business at Washington University, suggests that "Unlike the traditional regulating commissions which generally have jurisdiction over individual industries, these newer agencies cover virtually all companies, including many sectors of economic activity that are not generally thought of as being regulated by government." [18] Whereas the traditional regulatory agencies, such as the FCC and the ICC, were in charge of a specific industry or sector, the activities of the newer agencies are far more wide-ranging. Often the scope is so vast that the staff cannot possibly understand the unique problems of each industry or develop concern for the welfare of any particular sector of the economy. They follow no product through to completion, nor do they observe all aspects of a single company or business.

DISCLOSURE REGULATIONS: CONFLICT BETWEEN AGENCIES

The agencies that have been created recently are unlike the older agencies. The older ones have established routines and limits on their jurisdiction, though some of them, such as the SEC and the FTC, have become more aggressive and expanded their jurisdiction. The new commissioners of the agencies are often enthusiasts who believe they have a "cause" and push to expand their budget, workforce, and jurisdiction. In many cases, such an expansion is made without closely analyzing the cost to the government, or the far greater cost to consumers which must be absorbed when companies pass on the cost of compliance with new regulations. Virtually no cost-benefit analysis appears to have been undertaken before any new regulatory disclosure legislation, rules, or procedures are put into effect. The result is that corporations disclose volumes of facts and figures which no one is sure is necessary or useful.

ARMOUR MEATS: A CASE OF CONFLICT

Consider the plight of the Armour meat-packing plant, which was ordered by the Federal Meat Inspection Service to create an aperture in a sausage conveyor line so that inspectors could take out samples to test. The Company created the aperture. Along came the Occupational Safety and Health Administration and demanded that the aperture be closed, since it presented a potential safety hazard. Each agency threatened to shut down the plant if the company did not comply with its orders.[19]

However, the most devasting aspect of regulatory power has been its ability to delay or prevent the introduction of new products and the growth of new industries. For example, the Food and Drug Administration has delayed the introduction of new drugs, in many cases for four years or more, and thus has caused higher prices for pharmaceuticals and a delay in the availability of better therapies.[20]

COST-BENEFIT ANALYSIS OF DISCLOSURE REGULATIONS

President Ford, in November 1974, instructed those federal agencies under presidential jurisdiction to examine the effects of their disclosure requirements and major regulatory actions on cost, productivity, employment, and other economic factors. President Carter sought an analysis of the benefits gained from disclosure requirements and enforcement activity of all agencies. The Office of Management and Budget and the Congressional Budget Office are also concerned with determining when the costs of a disclosure program would exceed potential benefits for society. The key problem is how to measure costs and benefits and to make acceptable estimates. Many concur that, as difficult as it may be to measure benefits with a dollar amount, some clear cost-benefit analysis must be applied to the disclosure to prevent costs from exceeding benefits.

The argument put forth by William Sneath, chairman of the board of Union Carbide, for example, is echoed by countless members of the business community: "If it costs one hundred million dollars to clean up the air or water to 90% purity, and another one hundred to clean up the last 10%, then we ought to stop and carefully reassess just how important the last 10% really is."

Many are now willing to reexamine the balance of the costs against the merits of disclosure, which represents a significant change from the decade of the sixties, when *all* disclosure requirements were regarded favorably. As a result, government analysts are exploring various ways in which tax laws and credits might be used as incentives for voluntary disclosure and enforcement. This idea is still in its formative stages.

The failure or poor performance of certain so-called "over-regulated industries" has led to the ultimate question underlying cost-benefit tests of disclosure laws and compliance—namely, should such industries be "deregulated"?. The first reform of regulatory agencies came in 1978 when the airlines and the natural gas companies were deregulated. Proposals concering broadcast communication and truck transportation followed. This trend is expected to spread into the disclosure procedures of more federal agencies. For example, because of the extraordinary lobbying prowess of many industries and because of the increasing fears of a national energy crisis, enormous pressure was brought to bear on the Environmental Protection Agency to ease a number of water and air pollution rules and requirements, as well as others; this is expected to reduce some business costs of compliance by up to 40 percent.

OTHER PROBLEMS WITH REGULATORY AGENCIES

One of the classic attacks made upon the regulatory agencies by critics from the "left" is that the regulators and the industries they regulate are "in bed together." Indeed Victor Kramer examined the backgrounds of all appointees to nine regulatory commissions. He reported that in 30 percent of these cases, appointees came to the agencies from the very industries which they were supposed to regulate.[21] The advantage of such previous affiliation is that the regulators are cognizant of the difficulties confronting an industry. The danger is that they will not force the necessary disclosure or reforms. The question is whether the regulators, therefore, become captives of the industry they are to regulate. Apparently, President Carter agreed with this appraisal, because immediately upon entering office he introduced prohibitions to limit "revolving door" relationships, and by July of 1979 they were fully in effect.

The regulatory agencies also have rules that restrict the private employment of former senior government executives. For at least one year from the time they leave the government, a federal official may not represent private interests before any government agency with jurisdiction in any area in which the official had been involved. Many agencies have even more rigid rules and regulations regarding this immediate transfer of knowledge and influence from the pubic to the private sector. The Federal Power Commission and the Federal Trade Commission for example, prohibit former employees from testifying or being active in a case before the Commission.

DISCLOSURE AND THE NATURE OF THE AGENCIES

John Dunlop, the former Secretary of Labor, enumerated all other problems regulatory bodies have caused and, then, offered six solutions.[22]

First, regulatory agencies encourage simplistic thinking about complicated issues.

Second, although the task of writing and administering disclosure requirements is incredibly complex, the agencies frequently only add to the complexity, thus ensuring that obtaining compliance with their rules, procedures, and regulations becomes extraordinarily time consuming. Another result of this complexity of regulation is that it is virtually impossible to inform all affected parties of a new rule.

Third, unintended consequences of disclosure cause side effects with which regulators have to deal. For example, the Wagner Act had the effect of encouraging competition between unions for members. It thus forced a change in the internal governance of organized labor, which was an entirely unintended effect. (Article XX of the AFL-CIO Constitution was adopted to provide a method for mitigating these disputes through limited arbitration.)

Fourth, the rule-making and adjudicatory procedures or regulatory agencies tend to be very slow, creating conflicts between the different groups involved and leading to weak and ineffective remedies for the people the program aims to help. (The Administrative Procedure Act of 1946 was designed to establish formal procedures for the promulgation of rules and adjudication of cases so that each party affected by a proposed rule would have a chance to present its views, thereby limiting regulatory arbitrariness.)

Fifth, the rule-making and adjudicating procedures of agencies do not include a mechanism for the development of mutual accommodation among the conflicting interests. Opposing interests argue their case to the government, and not to each other. Public hearings encourage dramatic presentations and exorbitant demands. The regulatory agency is not aware of each party's true position, and must estimate priorities and needs from the formal and often extreme public statements the parties present at public hearings.

A sixth problem is that regulatory agencies and laws are rarely terminated after their purpose has been served. (There are exceptions, such as the Civil Aeronautics Board and Federal Communications Commission, and the new sunset laws are designed to repeal anachronistic laws and regulations.)

Seventh, legal game-playing is encouraged between regulators and businesses testing, tricking, bluffing, and accommodating, rather than resolving problems and conflicts in a straight-forward manner.

An eighth problem is that the small and medium-size firms are more adversely impacted by regulation.

Ninth, over time, the rule-making and disclosure activities become routine, and highly qualified staffs and effective administrators cannot be attracted.

Tenth, uniform federal regulations are inherently unworkable because the society is not uniform. For example, federal regulations have a different effect on small farms in the New England states than they do on the giant farms in the Midwest.

Eleventh, a number of different agencies share many of the same responsibilities and can cause conflict and confusion.

Dunlop offers six suggestions for improving the effectiveness of regulatory agencies.

First, affected parties should be involved in developing the regulations.

Second, anachronistic and unnecessary regulations should be repealed, future regulations and disclosure requirements should be promulgated with greater reluctance, and should have expiration dates.

Third, regulators should achieve compliance through consultation. The system of applying compulsion and fines simply has not proved successful. In fact, it has worked against acceptance of regulations by isloating the regulators and their expertise from those in business.

Fourth, coordination is needed among agencies.

Fifth, regulations must be made to reflect differences between industries and geographic regions.

Finally, all disclosure and regulatory agencies need to emphasize collective bargaining approaches.

CORPORATE MANAGERS CONFRONT A NEW SOCIETY

There seems little question these days that there is a demand for more disclosure from corporations, not only by government agencies, even beyond the stockholders, bondholders, and banks, employees, consumers, local community and special interest groups, even competitors are making these demands. For their part, most corporations, despite these social pressures, are not willing voluntarily to go beyond their legal obligations in disclosure.

CHAPTER 10

Liability and the Law

The public has come to feel that it is entitled to everything it needs to know to assess both the economic and societal performance of publicly held companies, especially in areas such as the environment and health. At the same time as this universal demand for corporate disclosure has been recognized, American society has gone to extremes to protect the individual's right to privacy. For instance, an employer is not totally free to ask the background of a potential employee if it would reveal racial, sexual, age, religious, or even some medical or criminal information. This right must be tempered by some well defined right of corporate privacy analogous to the individual privacy.

PUBLIC COMPANIES

The government view is that a public corporation gives up the right to much of its privacy when it goes public and sells stock. The pressures of disclosure have become so onerous that some managers have bought back all the publicly held shares of the company in an effort to make the company private again. For the most part, only small companies or those with relatively few shares outstanding could take such a step. Recently, however, Leonard N. Stern, the owner-manager of Hartz Mountain, the $250 million pet supply corporation, acquired back all the public shares of his company to become a private family company again.

Many corporations have resisted the loss of privacy and compliance with what "the public" seems to be seeking. However even though in legal terms the corporation is "a fictitious person," it does not have a right, in the abstract, to be left alone or a right to personal privacy. As one judge has summed it up:

What has developed in lieu of the open disclosure envisioned by Congress is a literary art form calculated to communicate as little of the essential information as possible while exuding an air of total candor. Masters of this medium utilize turgid prose to enshroud the occasional critical revelation in a morass of dull—and to all but the sophisticated—useless financial and historical data. In the face of such obfuscatory tactics the common or even well-informed investor is almost as much at the mercy of the issuer as was his pre-SEC parent.[1]

DISCLOSURE FORCES LITIGATION

It is clear that disclosure laws and disclosure agencies often lead straight to litigation in the courts. This stems partly from the mass of legislation pouring out of Congress and the state legislature, which some estimate at more than 150,000 new laws a year. Moreover, because disclosure laws are often enacted piecemeal and randomly, they sometimes overlap and conflict with one another. Litigation also has increased as a result of the passage of statutes which permit individuals to enforce "deferral law" without waiting for regulatory agencies to take action. These statutes provide what many call a new *private right of action.* These laws encourage individuals, environmental groups, and other affected parties, even those with very shaky or nonexistent claims to bring suit virtually without cost because the corporation, if it loses, must pay all legal expenses. Moreover, because of statutes which allow endless discovery proceedings, it is possible for an individual or group to prolong litigation and cripple a company with legal costs. This tactic is popular among persons suing corporations.

PERSONAL LIABILITY OF MANAGERS

In the last decade corporate managers and directors have been held personally liable for their corporate actions. For instance, if an officer of a company fails to obtain competitive bids for a major purchase, he may be held personally responsible in court. In general, should a corporate director or office act mistakenly or negligently—or fail to act at all when action is required—his personal assets may be at stake. Directors and officers have been held personally liable by courts for such acts as imprudent investment of corporate funds and failure to exercise reasonable care in the selection of a bank. As a result, directors and officers must be fully informed about the actions and policies of their company. In particular, directors should make a reasonable investigation at first hand, if need be, of the policies on which they deliberate as board members.

These policies may include such matters as corporate financing and financial reporting, issuing securities, proposed mergers and acquisitions, and the like. Corporate officers have specific responsibility to use *"reasonable care"* in overseeing the day-to-day activities of their company's employees.

Even though officers and directors may act objectively, and diligently, management is never totally immune from attack. Every act performed by a director or officer that could result in a loss of any kind should be viewed as a potential liability situation. For example, a suit was filed against Henry Ford which contended that he had "personal liability" for the defective design of the Ford Pinto because he or his company reputedly possessed test results in advance of fatal accidents indicating knowledge of these defects.

In the event of a suit, the "prudent man rule" may furnish a defense for the officer or director if it can be shown that he did everything an ordinary prudent man would have done. If he acted "in good faith" and "in the best interests of the company as he saw them," he will usually be reimbursed or indemnified by his company for any legal fees and judgments incurred. This is why 90 percent of firms listed in the New York Stock Exchange carry directors' and officers' liability insurance ranging from $5 million to $60 million.[2] (The premiums usually reflect the company's relative vulnerability to adverse litigation.)

What makes a company particularly susceptible to private litigation involving directors and officers can be sheer size, extensive government regulation of its operations, or years of unprofitable performance. Highly diversified companies are more prone to litigation than are single-purpose businesses, as are firms engaged in acquisition. Publicly held companies are more vulnerable than private or closely held companies, since stockholders frequently bring action against their own companies, as do employees and former employees, customers, and prior owners of acquired companies.

THE CORPORATE INTEREST

Today, corporations are hiring counsel to represent "the corporate interest," and experts envisage the gradual development of corporate legal committees to serve this purpose. This trend has been made necessary, in part, because the SEC has ruled that outside law firms which represent a company may no longer put a member on the board of the client company. The SEC reasons that a member of the board is a principal and there are obvious areas of potential conflict of interest. Harold

Williams, chairman of the SEC has urged law firms that serve as outside counsel to corporations to have second-partner review and assignment rotation to "minimize the natural blurring of objectivity which can result from long-standing personal and professional relationships between the clients managers and the partners." [3]

Inside counsel may run the risk of developing a "corporate dependence" and must instead develop "independence." They may tend to function only as legal technicians rather than as the vehicle through which the corporate conscience can be activitated. This tendency is encouraged by the fact that today's corporate lawyers must answer to directors and stockholders, the public, and government. To some, disclosure appears to be one means to assure that the corporate lawyers are not overlooking any unethical or illegal activities. For Harold Williams "Disclosure is a prophylactic. It prevents the birth of thousands of types of illegalities at their very moment of conception."

BUSINESS CRIME AND DISCLOSURE

White-collar crime in 1978 was estimated by the House Judiciary Committee to have cost the American public about $44 billion a year. In fact, the Committee branded white-collar crime the most serious, insidious crime problem in the United States. In that same year, the U.S. Chamber of Commerce and the Joint Congressional Economic Committee concurred that losses from white-collar crime, exclusive of illegal price-fixing and fraud against government programs, are more than 10 times the $4 billion annual cost for all street crimes against property. According the the late Senator Philip Hart (D., Mich.), if one adds the illegal price-fixing, corporate antitrust violations, and fraud against all government programs, the total cost approaches $200 billion a year.[4] Moreover, the total losses cannot be measured fully in terms of money, as the chairman of the House Judiciary Committee, John Conyers, Jr. (D., Mich.) concluded. A deeper loss involves cynicism, disrespect for law, and erosion of moral values.[5] It is because of the types of infraction mentioned above that additional regulatory agencies were organized to oversee corporate activity in the mid-seventies. By their vigilance they hope to prevent the continued increase of business and professional crimes.

White-collar crime includes crimes that are committed for one's personal benefit, such as tax or medicare frauds. The usual victims are individuals, businessess, and local, state, or the federal government. Business executives may try to further their own interests or those of their business by violating the laws. Some may seek enrichment at the expense of a company by embezzling funds. Some may bribe their customers' agents, use false weights, and measures, or misrepresent sales. The victims are the public and government. Some may commit fraud to cheat customers by trying to sell worthless securities, or business opportunities. The victims are the general public.

Unfortunately, white-collar crime, even after prosecution and conviction, is treated leniently because this type of crime does not employ violence and is, therefore, not regarded as being serious. The bank officer who lends the bank's assets on favorable terms to a business in which he has an interest or the businessman who pads expense accounts or invoices is not regarded as a criminal. In addition, some crimes are considered "justified" since government "doesn't understand" the needs of business. Many businessmen complain that government rules and standards are so numerous and strict that no one can meet them, and they say that, therefore, everyone can justify cheating "a little."

Examples abound of small business enterprises which pay "off the books" to avoid taxes, department heads who make excess payments to suppliers or who bribe city, state, state, or federal legislators, inspectors, or agency administrators. While to a degree such behavior always has been encountered and perhaps cannot be prevented, it is the extent of it today, as revealed by random sample studies carried out by government, university, and private research, that is truly alarming. Perhaps it should come as no surprise that in the last 10 to 15 years, government penalties, fines, and jail terms for regulatory offenses have been increasing, especially as a result of prosecutions by the SEC, the Federal Trade Commission, and the Occupational Safety and Health Administration.

An example of white-collar crime and its punishment is provided by the 1968 "Insiders case" of Texas Gulf Sulphur. Investigation of corporate, bank, government, and journalistic documents revealed that those involved in this case had passed along insider information to certain privileged stockholders that the company had made rich strikes of metal ore in its Canadian holdings. The defendants argued that their activities were common practice, an assessment that was perhaps correct. However, the government decided to make an example of this case and to enforce higher standards and new penalties. Numerous businessmen were found guilty and held personally liable.

Investigations using federal disclosure documents uncovered a case of long-term crime by 30 cardboard box manufacturers. They were found to have engaged in a 14-year conspiracy to fix prices, the longest price-fixing conspiracy in United States history. The attitude of the companies was that this had been simply business as usual. Although the antitrust division of the Justice Department had, for many decades, failed to punish this kind of crime, no such leniency was allowed this time. For the first time since the famous General Electric Price Fixing Case (1962), numerous executives were prosecuted, found guilty, sentenced to jail and fined. For example, the chief executive of Continental Can Company, one of the box manufacturers, along with 30 other executives of the other companies, was sentenced to jail and a fine of $100,000.

The SEC also required corporations which suspected their employees of illegal or questionable payments to undertake a careful examination of the facts in each case. If an investigation disclosed questionable or illegal acts, the corporations were advised to discuss them with the SEC before filling out any of the necessary documents. The SEC even went to the extent of writing guidelines for conducting such investigation. It specified that the probe should be made by "persons not involved in the activities in question." The investigators "should report and be responsible to a committee comprised of members of the board of directors who are not officers of that company and who were not involved in the suspected practices."

"Advice should be sought from independent public accountants and from outside legal counsel." The SEC also specified what should be done by the corporate managers and directors after they had completed their self-investigation. First, the special committee of investigation within the company should deliver to the company's board of directors a full report of its findings. Next, the SEC required that the external auditors investigate not only all the traditional areas of required disclosure, but the scope of each questionable or illegal act, the role of top management, how entries were made in the books, the existence of off-book accounts, foreign and domestic tax consequences, and finally, the effect of these illegal payments on the company's operations. Understandably these specifications created an uproar among accountants, who suddenly found themselves agents of the government looking over corporate records.

Not only does the SEC want questionable or illegal payments made public, but it now requires that companies report in proxy statements the involvement of top management in specified types of questionable or illegal corporate payments. In this way, the government is not only using its disclosure powers to bring illegal behavior to light, but also to force corporations to police themselves.

OTHER AGENCIES' DISCLOSURE REQUIREMENTS INVOLVING WHITE-COLLAR CRIME

While the SEC has issued most of the disclosure guidelines relating to white-collar crime, it is not the only agency to have done so. In October

1978, the Justice Department unveiled a new policy designed to encourage voluntary disclosure of antitrust violations which would give serious consideration to lenient treatment of corporations or officers who voluntarily reported their wrongdoing before it was discovered. As a result, regulatory agencies have been able to catch a number of wrongdoers. This voluntary system grew out of the SEC's decision to provide lenient treatment for Titanium Metals Corp. of America after that company's disclosure led to the indictment of four other titanium producers on charges of price-fixing. Although this type of legal "deal" is often made, the legal establishment claimed to be hesitant to adhere to such a policy publicly. In fact, the Justice Department continues to stress that leniency will not be "automatic" for companies that disclose price-fixing or other antitrust violations. The antitrust division of the Justice Department will be strongly influenced in deciding how lenient it will be with companies who voluntarily disclose their own wrongdoing, according to the following standards. The company is the first of a group of companies involved in a violation to disclose information about it. The disclosure is a truly corporate act, rather than the confession of individual executives or officials. The disclosure provides information that the Justice Department would not have learned from other sources. The Department also examines certain other factors, including the nature of a company's role in a violation, the candor of the disclosure, actions taken to terminate participation in the illegal activity, and its willingness to compensate those injured by the activity. One reason that Titanium Metals received lenient treatment was that it volunteered information to the antitrust division after initiating its own internal investigation and concluding that certain of its employees had been involved in illegal pricing discussions. (However, it took the Justice Department two years to agree to be lenient with wrongdoers who had cooperated.) Beyond the advantages of leniency, there are even more concrete benefits, namely, tax benefits for companies that cooperate with antitrust prosecutors. Companies convicted of price fixing can deduct one third of any treble-damage claims against it by private litigants.

Although the SEC has been lenient with companies that disclose wrongdoing, corporate executives are still aware of the fact that jail sentences are being levied on offenders. The sentences have nearly doubled, to 2921 days for 29 individuals in 1978 from 1561 days for 24 individuals only one year earlier. This increase is a signal to all corporate executives, managers, and directors that the Justice Department means business. It has won 14 of the 15 felony price-fixing cases that have come to trial since 1974. Shenefield is not exaggerating when he argues, "The risk of conviction, fines and jail sentences following indictment is approaching a certainty."

PERKS

Although disclosure requirements seem to be onerous to businessmen, they strike others as less than adequate in forcing businessmen to reveal all their activities and the true nature of their business dealings. For example, the SEC's new requirement for disclosure of all corporate benefits provided to employees reflects the belief that hidden bonuses and perquisites have become so sizeable that in some cases they equal an executive's compensation. Henceforth, the five highest paid directors or all executive officers who receive more than $50,000 a year will have to report earnings including direct and indirect compensation (stock options and bonuses). The SEC also is looking into special loans that corporations facilitate for their executives.

CHAPTER 11

The Limits of Disclosure

MATERIALITY: THE BASIS OF DISCLOSURE

Under their terms of incorporation, companies are legally bound to disclose certain information to the government and must often report to trade associations, industry groups, and securities markets. The nature and extent of the information disclosed is governed by the concept of "materiality." Essentially, materiality limits the amount of data that a company must disclose, since full disclosure is impractical, undesirable and, often impossible.

A traditional standard of materiality defines facts necessary in disclosure as those which would change the mind or decisions of the "average individual" in, for example, making an investment or a purchase. The courts have attempted to determine which facts would affect the decision-making process of an individual. Some decisions have held that information must be disclosed which "would have an impact," "might have an impact," or "might have a significant propensity to impact" on the decision-making process. The Supreme Court has enunciated a different degree of certainty. For a fact to be material, there must be a "substantial likelihood that the omitted fact would have assumed actual significance in the deliberations of the reasonable man."

In another Supreme Court decision, Affiliated Citizens v. the United States (1972), the court stated: "All that is necessary is that the facts withheld be material in the sense that a reasonable investory might have considered them important in the making of his decision."

However, in the case of Mills v. Electric Auto-Lite Company (1974), the Court refused to consider the issue of materiality. The Court did enunciate a separate standard of materiality by stating, in effect, that a fact is material if it has a significant propensity to affect the decision-making process of the reasonable investor.

The TSC Industries v. Northway, Inc. case clarified the standard by

105

which materiality should be judged. The Court analyzed the various standards of materiality and stated that the "purpose is not merely to ensure by judicial means that the transaction, when judged by its real terms, is fair and otherwise adequate, but to ensure disclosure by corporate management in order to enable the shareholders to make an informed choice."

ACCOUNTING AND DISCLOSURE REQUIREMENTS

According to the Securities and Exchange Commission's definition of audit, "a public accountant's examination is intended to be an independent check upon management's accounting of its stewardship." Thus the auditor has a "direct and unavoidable responsibility of his own, particularly where his engagement relates to a company which makes filings with the commission or in which there is a substantial public interest." Accountants must assure that businesses comply with the statutes and regulations, as well as verify records and reports and provide tax management advice. Yet, for a number of reasons, accounting professionals believe that the accounting profession should never have been required to assume these responsibilities. The first reason concerns the question of whether disclosure makes any difference to investors and markets. More than a decade of academic research was conducted on the "efficient market hypothesis," which assumes that security values reflect all information available to the public and to sophisticated investors. Research indicated that the market is not fooled by accounting changes used to increase reported earnings, such as a switch from straight line to accelerated depreciation. Accountants concluded that vast amounts of new disclosure requirements might not help investors and simply would impose extra burdens upon companies. The second reason accountants do not feel they should be responsible for disclosure is the fact that the SEC has assumed jurisdiction for corporate disclosure. A third reason accountants have become reluctant to assume responsibility for disclosure is the fact that many companies resist increased disclosure requirements and the accompanying costs.

A final and more pervasive reason has been a general disillusionment with governmental regulation in all areas of the economy.

Yet, the SEC, unmoved by the protests, also has instituted a requirement that companies disclose the replacement cost of inventories, plant, and equipment in Accounting Series Release 190 (1976). The addition, the approximate cost of sales based on the replacement cost of inventories at the time sales were made and of the amount of replacement cost based on depreciation, depletion, and amortization on properties owned were to be disclosed.

The SEC has expanded interim reporting requirements for Form 10-Q and has instituted requirements for reporting quarterly operating results (ASR 177) in annual reports. The so-called "preferability" feature which requires that a firm's independent auditors indicate whether a change in the firm's accounting methods (other than one dictated by an FASB pronouncement) is, in their judgment, a switch to a "preferable" method. Public accounting firms were virtually unanimous in their opposition to the "preferability" requirement. Arthur Anderson & Company went further than merely voicing protests and mounted a legal challenge, but the challenge was dismissed by a Chicago judge.

IMPLICATIONS FOR ACCOUNTING OF NEW DISCLOSURE

An Advisory Committee on Corporate Disclosure has raised questions of legal liability for the accounting profession. Forecast data will be one of the key targets. The concept of "differential disclosure," as well as the implementation of a two-tier reporting scheme are also under study. While each of these proposals poses legal risks of liability for accountants, the future is not all bleak for the accounting profession. Accountants' liability will be substantially reduced if the SEC's proposal goes into effect. This proposal would reduce the number of "significant categories of events" which must be reported in the monthly 8-K filings. In addition, "streamlining" of SEC disclosure requirements would reduce accountants' liability. However, reductions would be balanced against new pressures to increase the liability of all accounting, legal, and financial advisors.

Rule 10b5 of the Securities Exchange Act of 1934 is important to any discussion of the legal liability of accountants, as well as of managers, lawyers, and financial advisors. Under the heading Employment of Manipulative and Deceptive Devices, it states:

It shall be unlawful for any person, directly or indirectly, by the use of any means or instrumentality, of interstate commerce, or of the mails, or of any facility of a national securities exchange:
1. To employ any device, scheme or artifice to defraud.
2. To make any untrue statement of a material fact necessary to make the statements made, in the light of the circumstances under which they were made, not misleading.
3. To engage in any act, practice or course of business which oper-

ates or would operate as a fraud or deceit upon any person, in connection with the purchase or sale of any security.

It is under this rule that the most famous and significant cases involving financial reporting systems have been brought. For example the Westec, Continental Vending, Barchris cases all stemmed from these SEC rules and required the courts to interpret the meaning of such terms in Rule 10 b 5 as "material fact," "misleading" and "in the light of the circumstances."

Accountants have attempted to counter the risk to their profession by having lawyers cite the more established legal principles of the "common law defenses." Although it may yet prove to be ineffective, the argument was at least partially successful in the recent case of Hochfelder v. Ernst and Ernst. The ruling did not impose total liability on accounting auditors for negligence; rather, it assigned liability only where intent to defraud or act illegally was involved.

Several studies have argued that the liability of auditors should be decreased, given the new widespread acceptance of the efficient market hypothesis. Ball and Brown, in 1968, and Ball, in 1972, showed that the information contained in financial reports has largely been gathered before the auditors make their report, thereby suggesting that there is some alternative source of information. If relevant information is always provided by some competing source and the market is able to discern correct information, then fraudulent, mistaken, or negligent accounting information could not mislead the buyers. Were this true, the potential liability of accountants should be reduced. However, James Anderson concluded that buyers in the security market have been fooled by the failure of the corporations to make timely disclosure of relevant information, and the effectiveness of alternative sources of information has been inadequate.

Under common law, accountants traditionally had a contractual obligation to the corporate client to perform specified tasks according to the standards of their profession. Negligence by an auditor prompted suits by the corporate client, not the investors. With rare exceptions, the auditors were not linked contractually to the investors and, therefore, were shielded from either individual or class-action suits. Today however, auditors are not protected from individual suits, and shareholders can complain of breach of the standard of due care and diligence. This came about as a result of a 1968 case, Ranch Factors Inc. v. Levin. The decision in this case reversed the Ultramares decision. The Cartier Ultramares decision expressed the "foreseeability" rule which limited accountants', lawyers' and financial advisors' legal duty to protect third parties or those who did not sign the contract that employed the accountant. It also established the principle of liability for deceit of third parties, including stockholders. In Ultramares the court said:

> If liability for negligence exists, a thoughtless slip or blunder, the failure to detect a theft or forgery beneath the cover of deceptive entries, may expose accountants to a liability in an indeterminate amount for an indeterminate time to an indeterminate class. The hazards of a business conducted on these terms are so extreme as to enkindle doubt whether a flaw may not exist in the implication of a duty that exposes one to these consequences.

The Rosch case also made accountants and financial advisors liable for negligence *and* established the right of noncontracting parties to sue auditors, lawyers, and all other financial advisors. Then, in 1976, the Hochfelder case, which sought to make auditors originally liable for simple negligence in preparing a company's financial statement was tried. Ultimately, the Supreme Court declined to extend criminal liability to a case of auditors' simple negligence. The Court stated that the acceptance of Hochfelder's view would extend to new frontiers the "hazards" of rendering expert advice under the acts, raising serious probing questions not yet addressed by Congress. It had to be proved that intent was involved, the court concluded, in order to prove criminal negligence on the part of expert advisors. However, in the footnotes to the Hochfelder case, the court stated that recklessness should be considered to be a form of intentional conduct for purposes of imposing liability for some act. Consequently, it seems clear from this decision, and from various other court judgments, that financial and legal advisors are not protected from liability merely because they are unaware of a fraudulent act, or do not intend to deceive.

Who are these people or classes of people who can reasonably claim injury? At first it would seem to be practically anyone who might claim to be a potential investor. Yet, legally, the injured are limited to those who can demonstrate that they relied on false and misleading information. Many investors perhaps would have bought the securities even if they were aware of the falsity or mistaken character of the accounting reports. Justifiable reliance is, therefore, strictly defined as a causal connection between the wrongful conduct and the resulting damage. Yet, although the law sets up these tests and strict definitions to limit those who can bring claims, it should be clear that by opening the door to such claims the potential legal responsibility for negligence will become far greater and the traditional common law defense against negligence will become weaker.

Auditors and lawyers are considered to be experts who can be held to a higher standard of professional competence than some other professionals. They are expected to take greater care and, as a result, are considered to be more liable for negligence involving reckless disregard of the truth than would be an ordinary citizen.

CHAPTER 12

Corporate Governance

Public distrust of and alienation from corporations has been fostered by events as diverse as corporate payoff scandals and Watergate, soaring inflation and gas shortages, as well as the growing size and power of institutions such as giant bureaucratic government and multinational corporations. One consequence of this sentiment has been strident demands from social interest groups and newly created—or revitalized—government agencies for corporate social responsibility as well as strict accountability of individual managers. The demands extend to composition of board of directors and committees to the composition of products, the workforce, and of the geographic, moral, and political nature of investments.

The central thrust of this movement toward corporate governance focuses directly upon the fundamental philosophic questions concerning who should own, direct, and control production in America, and to whom are corporate managers ultimately responsible. That is, managers still seek to maximize profits and growth and to respond to stockholders. What has changed is the amount of time and energy these managers must devote to an increasing number of constituencies. Not only are there stockholders, there are stakeholders as well, including employees (with their pension funds), customers, local community groups, national, state and local government, consumers, and the public at large. In addition, because decisions concerning resource allocation are of the greatest consequence to the public welfare, corporate executives have come to realize their responsibility to conserve scarce resources.

Derek Bok, President of Harvard, has described the role expected of executives.

Management exists not simply to serve shareholders but to exercise leadership in reconciling the needs of stockholders, customers, em-

111

ployees and suppliers, along with members of the public and their representatives in government. Indeed, many executives today feel increasingly moved not only to further the interests of their company but to defend the entire free enterprise system by participating visibly in efforts to save the inner cities, train the hard-core unemployed, improve the educational system, and address other major social ills.[1]

Unlike business managers, the men responsible for administering financial institutions, such as banks, brokerage firms, mutual funds, and pension funds, are notorious for their reluctance to disclose any information about their firms. As a result, the Pension Rights Reform Center was established in 1976 to educate the American public about retirement income and to provide technical assistance to pension plan participants and beneficiaries. But there are other problems. In a recent panel discussion on corporate governance, Dan Krausse, president and chief executive officer of Earth Resources Company, revealed that his company had been frustrated in efforts to reach "blind" investors of the company, such as stock held in "street name" and by indirect investors, in order to communicate information. Merrill, Lynch, Pierce, Fenner and Smith had 7000 customers who were blind investors of Earth Resources and refused to give the Company this mailing list or act as a conduit for distributing the information. This financial institution also discouraged the company representatives from attempts to increase shareholder participation. Jay Tolson, president and chairman of the Fisher and Porter Company—at the same conference—emphasized that "companies should have a right and an obligation to reach their shareholders.[2] Nevertheless, managers at financial institutions have pointed out that laws governing rights of privacy prevented them from giving the names of investors to outsiders.[3]

While 75 percent of the respondents in one study indicate that the companies in which they are invested provide adequate information about their activities and policies, 67 percent of respondents in the same study agree that there is a need for a mechanism other than stockholder relations departments and annual meetings, to enable them to communicate with management. However, 35 percent of those who agree gave an emphatic "yes" and 32 percent answered "sometimes."

The degree of confidence investors have in the ability of several different types of institutions to act as corporate watchdogs and serve as sources for disclosure to the public was also measured. Accounting and CPA firms are on the top, with a 64 percent approval rating, and government agencies—using the example of the SEC—are next with a 56 percent confidence rating. The yes and no votes are split almost in half for and against confidence in the ability of the business-press and media to handle corporate disclosure, and law firms received only 21 percent approval as watch dogs on sources of disclosure.

REPORT OF THE AMERICAN ASSEMBLY ON CORPORATE GOVERNANCE

The interest in corporate governance is growing, and as one result, a group met to consider the impact of corporate governance on the society.[4] The group concluded that shareholders, as the undisputed owners of corporations, possess great potential influence to make management and directors aware of social and economic issues. The shareholders should insist, for example, that the majority of board members should come from outside corporate management, unencumbered by relationships which could limit their independence. The function of the chairman of the board should be made independent of the chief executive officer, however, key inside managers, in addition to the chief executive officer, should remain eligible to serve. The board needs a clear definition of its role and functions. Committee structures, responsibilities, and relationship to the full board should be spelled out. The key committees should include the nominating, audit, compensation, and public (or social) issues committees. The nominating, audit, and compensation committees should be composed entirely of independent directors. The public issues committee should have at least a majority of independent directors.

Corporations should disclose detailed information relating to the membership, selection, and processes of the board of directors. The nominating committee should establish standards for evaluating directors' performance and recommend to the board dismissal of ineffective directors. Shareholders, subject to reasonable qualifications, should have the right to nominate directors and have their nominees included in proxy statements of the corporation.

The audit committee should recommend an independent auditor to the board, review the scope of the audit, and set the fee. Audit fees should be disclosed to shareholders, and the choice of auditors should be ratified by shareholders. The audit committee should meet with the independent auditing firm, and some portion of each meeting should be conducted without internal staff or other members of management present.

To meet the inquiries of the stockholders, corporations should set up committees to evaluate public issues as well as their own business practices and use the results to alter policy as necessary to serve public concerns. The advisory committees should include employees as well as, for example, consumers and environmentalist. Corporations also should hold open meetings with public groups to discuss social and business issues and related corporate performance. In addition, trade associations could help educate their corporate members in identifying public concerns and emerging public demands.

A concrete approach to assessing the degree to which a company is responding to social responsibility is the social audit. In concept, it is a detailed account of every social accomplishment of a company and it serves as a method for indicating progress either in a particular area of social importance or across the board. The audit, in fact, takes social responsibility out of the realm of abstraction and connects it directly with the bottom line—in dollar-and-cent terminology. It also measures social goals as they relate to or break with overall objectives of the business. In short, it brings social responsibility up to—or down to—the same level as financial responsibility.

Many large companies are now publishing such audits in their annual reports and in booklets for public distribution. In 1953 Howard Bowen first proposed that businesses should conduct a social audit as a means of reporting its public activities and measuring its public response to social responsibility. This movement towards corporate social audits has now progressed so far that John Corson and George Steiner have identified five different approaches to making a business social audit.[5] The social programs of the company should be described. Potential additional social programs should be discussed. This approach is one of the widely used techniques.

Expenditures which have been made for social programs should be announced. General Motors, for example, evaluates its costs to improve its human assets, or the capability of the company's human organization, shareholder loyalty, and banker or community good will, and customer loyalty, among other things. The Barry Company of Columbus, Ohio, is one of the few to use this approach and combine such valuation with traditional financial reports. All companies should appraise the costs and effectiveness of those activities they have undertaken voluntarily for social reasons. In addition, management should be open and responsive to inquiries by the press, radio, and television on behalf of the public. The last point is worth special note. Fundamentally, the image of any corporation in the public eye will be affected by the way the media presents news about that corporation. That image, in turn, will relate directly to the perceived need for government intervention or regulation.

It would be wise for managers to assess the feasibility for implementing a social audit in their company, and to devise a plan of implementation. Voluntary action will prevent any mandatory action by government and respond to the obvious expectations of constituents. Currently, there is no standard to determine the response of business to the needs of society but there are efforts under way to establish one.

CHAPTER 13

Conclusion

The troubled confluence of business, media and the law reflects the demands that society imposes on each of these institutions to respond to change and to meet popular expectations. Business is expected to furnish goods and services at reasonable prices, generate a profit on business operations, and to discharge a certain social responsibility to employees, consumers, and the general public. The media, insofar as they constitute business, are expected to behave as responsible business organizations. They are charged with the special responsibility of reporting and interpreting to the public important news developments that occur in business, government and politics, and among the normal course of events. Legal and governmental institutions incur the obligation to protect society from abusive power and provide services that society cannot obtain from any other source.

Expectations in American society today are very high—for clean air and water, ethical government, and a healthy economy. Especially with respect to the economy, frustration is high over expectations not met. The media are expected, for example, to explain why oil prices are high and periodic gasoline shortages are predicted, why government is not sufficiently effective to tame supposed business avarice. Not surprisingly, those whose performances come under attack or question defend their performances, often by counterattacking.

Our institutions of government, media, and business are not inherently bad. They respond, for the most part, to change and meet the needs of people as no other institutions have in the past. In spite of this, they are seen by large segments of the public as increasingly remote; separate from one another and from those they serve. Thus, business must strive to regain public trust and credibility, as well as the respect of its adversaries. Ultimately public opinion is the court of last resort in a free society. Communications between the various participants in the conflict

116

are opening, and greater understanding will be the inevitable result. After a conference on business and media relations, Washington Post Editor Ben Bradlee remarked:

> I detect the beginnings of a thaw. I asked John deButts for his private telephone number, and damned if he didn't give it to me. I look on people with whom I had been supposed to be fighting with greater understanding and respect. Not love mind you. There is no room for love in the relationship between business and the press. Love breeds deception both ways, and everyone loses in that situation, mostly the public whom we both serve.

However, businessmen may have to be educated to be more accessible. As Frank Shakespeare has pointed out:

> In business it has been my observation that the chief executive officers of major corporations tend to be inhibited by the process by which they went to the top. They got there by being able, working hard and keeping their head down and not getting in trouble. . . . If we are in a real societal ferment about the role of government, limitation of government, degree of taxation, government regulation, private enterprise, socialism, about all of these questions, part of the leadership of a free society has to come from business leaders. . . . The chief executive officer not only sets the rules for himself, but he sets the parameters for his entire corporation, all of his junior managers. If he is afraid of a bad editorial, or a tough comment on the network and he keeps his head down, that whole corporation keeps its head down and a voice is lost, a tough, argumentative, additive voice to the American system.

Those who have risen to the top of major corporations must learn the business of the press, for they must rely upon the press to impress government agencies, legislative bodies, and local municipal groups—not just employees or shareholders. Executives must respond to media requests for information and learn to accept the media as a positive force for better communications. Former President Ford recently advised:

> You've got to be aggressive, factual, candid and straight-forward. Do that in the business community and you'll be a lot better off than sitting back and saying, that damn newspaper, that lousy government agency.

In turn, the news media must begin to recognize the objectives of business firms. If they are to cover business news accurately, journalists must comprehend the complexities and the technicalities of business. No doubt journalists will continue to be skeptical, but they should try to understand the constraints these complexities and technicalities impose on businessmen.

Lawmakers and regulatory authorities also must understand more fully the nature of business enterprises. The cost of compliance and cost-benefit analyses must be calculated to assure efficient and effective regulation. John de Butts summed up the challenge and the reward:

> We must be willing to face each other, to answer each other's questions as openly and candidly and honestly as we know how, admitting if we don't know the answer that we don't know the answer, saying forthrightly if it is something that we do not feel we can disclose, that we have it, but we cannot disclose it—as the press does on occasion. If all of us will try—business, media and government—then I think all of us will be a whole lot happier with the results.

Notes

CHAPTER 1

1. Alan F. Westin, "Ideas and Trends", *Business Week,* May 14, 1979, p. 14.
2. Ibid.
3. Sandy Socolow, NYU/FACS Conference, September 27, 1978.
4. *The Washington Star,* editorial, March 5, 1979.
5. "The Swarming Lobbyists", *Time* August 7, 1978.
6. William Sneath, *Dun's Review,* April, 1979, p. 117-119.
7. Frank Shakespeare NYU/FACS Conference, September 28, 1978.
8. Rear Admiral David M. Cooney, USN, speech at U.S. Naval Academy, Annapolis, Maryland, May, 1979.
9. Frank Shakespeare, NYU/FACS Conference, September 28, 1978.
10. David M. Rubin, "When the Press Puts the Pressure on Business," *Management Review,* February 1973.
11. Edward J. Walsh, "Why the Media Distrust Business," *Cleveland Magazine,* September 1977, p. 95.
12. Peter Drucker, "Good Growth and Bad Growth", *The Wall Street Journal,* April 10, 1979.

CHAPTER 2

1. Sylvia Chase, NYU/FACS Conference, September 27, 1978.
2. Alan L. Otten, "Politics and People," *The Wall Street Journal,* September 28, 1978.
3. Tom Brokaw, FACS Conference, November 18, 1977.
4. Rear Admiral David M. Cooney, USN, speech at U.S. Naval Academy, Annapolis, Maryland, May, 1979.
5. Les Whitten, NYU/FACS Conference, September 27, 1978.
6. Otten, op. cit.

7. Louis Banks, "Memo To The Press: They Hate You Out There," *Atlantic Monthly*, April, 1978.

CHAPTER 3

1. Christopher H. Sterling, and Timothy R. Haight, *The Mass Media: Aspen Institute Guide to Communication Industry Trends* (New York: Praeger Publishers, 1978), p. 49.
2. Frank Shakespeare, NYU/FACS Conference, September 28, 1978.
3. Lance Morrow, *Time,* "The Politics of the Box Populi," June 11, 1979.
4. Ibid.
5. Sterling, op. cit., p. 207.
6. Alan F. Westin, "Ideas and Trends," *Business Week,* May 14, 1979, p. 14.
7. Morrow, op. cit.
8. Thomas Griffiths, *Fortune,* "Must Business Fight the Press?" June, 1974, p. 203.
9. Bill Scott, NYU/FACS Conference, September 27, 1978.
10. Tom Brokaw, FACS Conference, November 18, 1977.
11. Robert Flaherty, NYU/FACS Conference, September 27, 1978.
12. S. Prakash Sethi, "Business and the News Media: The Paradox of Informed Misunderstanding, *California Management Review,* Spring 1977.
13. Arthur R. Taylor, "Why Business Got a Bad Name," *Business and Society Review,* No. 17-20, December 1977.
14. Virgil Dominic, letter to *Cleveland Plain Dealer,* March 8, 1977.
15. Harry Stein, "How 60 Minutes Makes News," *The New York Times Magazine,* May 6, 1979.
16. Ibid.
17. Sterling, op. cit., p. 43.
18. Ibid., p. 207.
19. Ibid., p. 19.
20. Frank Shakespeare, NYU/FACS Conference, September 28, 1978.
21. Frank Shakespeare, NYU/FACS Conference, September 28, 1978.
22. R. B. Pitkin, "An Analysis of the News Media," *American Legion Magazine,* March, 1970.
23. Robert Flaherty, op. cit.
24. Irving Kristol, NYU/FACS Conference, September 27, 1978.
25. Ben Bradlee, NYU/FACS Conference, September 27, 1978.
26. David Laventhol, NYU/FACS Conference, September 28, 1978.
27. Flaherty, op. cit.
28. Rubin, op. cit.
29. Ibid.
30. Diedre Carmody, *The New York Times* September 23, 1979.
31. Dorothy Brooks, NYU/FACS Conference, September 27, 1978.

CHAPTER 4

1. Arthur R. Taylor, "Why Business Got a Bad Name," *Business and Society Review,* No. 17-20, December 1977, p. 20.
2. Edward J. Walsh, "Why The Media Distrusts Business," *Cleveland Magazine,* September 1977, p. 100.
3. William E. Simon, *A Time For Truth,* (New York:McGraw Hill, 1978).
4. Walsh, op. cit.
5. S. Prakash Sethi, "Business and the News Media: The Paradox of Informed Misunderstanding," *California Management Review,* Spring 1977, p. 53.
6. Martin L. Gibson, "The Public Thinks We Slant the News," *The Bulletin of the American Society of Newspaper Editors,* September 1972, p. 17.
7. IABC *News* (International Association of Business Communicators) cited in FACS brochure, "Media 77," FACS Conference, November 18, 1977.
8. *Antitrust Law Review,* 1976-1977.
9. *The Wall Street Journal*
10. Sethi, op. cit., p. 54.
11. Taylor, op. cit., p. 19.
12. Sethi, op. cit., p. 53.
13. Simon, op. cit.
14. Ibid.
15. Louis Banks, "Memo to the Press: They Hate You Out There," *Atlantic Monthly,* April 1978, p. 37.
16. David M. Rubin, "When the Press Put Pressure on Business," *Management Review,* February 1973.
17. "Business and the Media," *Dun's Review,* May 1977, p. 18.
18. Frank Shakespeare, NYU/FACS Conference, September 28, 1978.
19. John F. Steiner, "The Business Response to Public Distrust," *Business Horizons,* April 1979.
20. Malcolm S. Forbes, "Fact and Comment," *Forbes Magazine,* May 28, 1979, p. 25.

CHAPTER 5

1. Tom Brokaw, FACS Conference, November 18, 1977.
2. George Heinemann, NYU/FACS Conference, September 27, 1978.
3. *Dun's Review,* "Business and the Media," May 1977, p. 76.
4. Ibid.
5. Robert Bartley, NYU/FACS Conference, September 27, 1978.
6. Flaherty, op. cit.
7. Katherine Graham, "Business and the Press," *University of Michigan Business Review,* January, 1976, p. 24.

8. Irving Kristol, "The Underdeveloped Profession," *The Public Interest*, No. 6, Winter 1967, p. 36.
9. Ibid.

CHAPTER 6

1. Charles W. Barry, letter to *Cleveland Press* July 10, 1979.
2. Robert S. Mason, "What's a PR Director For, Anyway?" *Harvard Business Review*, September-October 1974, p. 121.
3. Ibid, p. 125.
4. "The Corporate Image: P.R. To The Rescue," *Business Week*, January 22, 1979, p. 60.
5. Ibid.
6. Ibid.
7. Davis Young, speech to International Association of Business Communicators, Cleveland, Ohio, Chapter, April 11, 1979.
8. Craig Aronoff, "Credibility of Public Relations for Journalists," *The Public Relations Review*, August 1975, pp. 53-54.
9. Ibid.
10. Sylvia Chase, NYU/FACS Conference, September 27, 1978.
11. Tom Brokaw, "Media 77," Houston, Texas.
12. Reg Laite, NYU/FACS Conference, September 27, 1978.

CHAPTER 7

1. Arthur Brewster, Herbert Palmer, and Robert Ingraham, *Introduction to Advertising* New York: McGraw-Hill, 1954, p.9.
2. Ibid. p. 8.
3. Harold Nelson and Dwight Teeter, *Law of Mass Communications*, The Foundation Press, Mineola, N.Y.: p. 427.
4. Brewster, Palmer, and Ingraham, op. cit., p. 34.
5. Steven Simmons, "Commercial Advertising and the Fairness Doctrine: The New F.C.C. Policy in Perspective," *Columbia Law Review*, May-December 1975, p. 1085, n. 2225.
6. Gerald Grotta, Earnest Larkin, and Bob Carrell, "News Vs Advertising: Does the Audience Perceive The 'Journalistic Distinction'?" *Journalism Quarterly* Autumn 1976, p. 448.
7. Ibid., p. 448.
8. Ibid.
9. Lee Becker, Raymond Martino, and Wayne Towers, "Media Advertising Credibility," *Journalism Quarterly*, Summer 1976.
10. Bernard Rubin, ed., *Big Business and the Mass Media*, D.C. Heath & Co., Lexington, Mass: 1977, p. 27, note 70.
11. Lee Loevinger, "The Attack on Advertising and the Goals of Regulations," *Conference Board Record*, January, 1973, p. 2.

12. Ibid., p. 27.
13. R.A. Bauer and S.A. Greyser, "Advertising in America: The Consumer View," *Journal of Advertising,* November 1972, p. 11, Note 4.
14. Loevinger, op. cit., p. 23, n. 2.
15. "Madison Avenue's Response to Its Critics," *Business Week,* June 10, 1972, p. 46.
16. John K. Galbraith, *Economics and the Public Purpose,* Signet and Mentor Books, New York: 1975, p. 134-5.
17. *Business Week,* op. cit.
18. Miles W. Kirkpatrick, "Advertising and the Federal Trade Commission," *Journal of Advertising,* November 1973, p. 101.
19. Ibid., p. 435.
20. Loevinger, op. cit., p. 25.
21. Richard A. Posner, *Regulation of Advertising by the FTC* (Washington, D.C.: American Enterprise Institute for Public Policy Research).
22. Gerald J. Thain, "Advertising Regulations: The Contemporary FTC Approach", *Fordham Urban Law Journal,* Vol. 1 (1972-1973), p. 361, n. 29.
23. Branzhaf v. FCC 132, U.S. App. D.C. 14, 405 F2d 1802 (1968).
24. A.F. Ehrbar, "The Backlash Against Business Advocacy," *Fortune,* July 1978, p. 49.
25. "The Regulation of Corporate Image Advertising," *Minnesota Law Review* (1974-1975), p. 192.
26. Ibid., p. 189, n. 2.
27. William Sachs and Joseph Chasin, "Executives View Corporate Advertising," *Public Relations Journal,* November 1976.
28. Sylvan Barnet, *Public Relations Journal* November 1975, pp. 18-19.
29. Albert Stridsberg, "How to Organize Controversy Advertising," *Public Relations Journal,* November 1976, p. 24.
30. Donald W. Jugenheimer, "How to Evaluate Corporate Advertising," *Public Relations Journal,* November 1976, pp. 24.
31. Rubin, op. cit., p. 34.
32. Sethi, S. Prakash, "Issue-Oriented Corporate Advertising," *California Management Review,* Fall, 1976, p. 6.

CHAPTER 8

1. Weidenbaum, Working Paper, Center For the Study of American Business, St. Louis, July 1978, p. 4.
2. Harold L. Nelson and Dwight L. Teeter, *Law of Mass Communications,* (Mineola, N.Y.: Foundation Press, 1969), p. 14.
3. Edward Denison, *Survey of Current Business,* January 1978.
4. "Government Intervention," *Business Week,* April 4, 1977.
5. M.L. Erickson, T.W. Dunfee, and F.F. Gibson, *Antitrust and Trade Regulation* (Columbus, Ohio: Grid, Inc., 1977), p. 2.
6. T.W. Dunfee and F.F. Gibson, *Modern Business Law,* p. 29.

CHAPTER 9

1. Ronald A. Anderson, *Government and Business* New Rochelle, N.Y.: Southwestern Publishing, 1966, p. 374.
2. FDIC: Federal Deposit Insurance Corporation. SEC: Securities and Exchange Commission. FCC: Federal Communications Commission. CAB: Civil Aeronautics Board.
3. 10 percent changed to 5 percent.
4. "Is the SEC Going Too Far Too Fast?" *Business Week,* November 27, 1978.
5. See John G. Gillis "Securities Law and Corporate Disclosures, *Financial Analysts Journal,* January 1976; Ray Garrett, "Disclosure Rules and Annual Reports: Present Impact," *Financial Executive,* April, 1975, p. 20.
6. Gillis, op. cit., p. 18.
7. Homer Kripke, NYU/FACS Conference, September 28, 1978.
8. "Is the SEC Going Too Far Too Fast?" *Business Week,* November 27, 1978.
9. R. Corley, R. Black and O. Reed, *The Legal Environment of Business* (New York: McGraw Hill, 1963), p. 546.
10. "Business Backlash: More Companies Bar Regulating Agencies From Factories, Files," *Wall Street Journal* January 19, 1978, p. 1.
11. Ibid.
12. Ibid.
13. Jay Palmer, "The Rising.Risk of Regulation," *Time,* November 27, 1978.
14. Weidenbaum, Working Paper, p. 2.
15. Palmer, op. cit.
16. Ibid.
17. Weidenbaum, Working Paper, p. 4.
18. Ibid., p. 15.
19. William E. Simon, *A Time For Truth* (New York: McGraw-Hill, 1978), p. 182.
20. Ibid., p. 28.
21. Weidenbaum, *Business Government and the Public,* p. 7.
22. Dunlop, *The Conference Board Record,* March 1976.

CHAPTER 10

1. John J. McCloy, "American Bar Association Committee on Law and the Economy," *The New York Times,* August 9, 1978.
2. Insurance Company of North America Booklet.
3. "Is the SEC Going Too Far Too Fast?" *Business Week,* November 27, 1978.
4. "Drive to Curb Kickbacks and Bribes by Business," *U.S. News & World Report,* September 4, 1978, p. 41-5.
5. Ibid.

CHAPTER 12

1. Derek Bok, "The President's Report 1977-1978," Harvard University.
2. "Corporate Responsibility: Issue of the 80's," Panel Discussion at Conference held June 4-5, 1979, Growth Companies: Opportunity And Challenge, by U.S. Chamber of Commerce, Washington, D.C.
3. Karolyn R. Morigi, "Corporate Governance And The Individual Investor," Master's Thesis (1980).
4. "Corporate Governance In America," American Assembly Conference, April 13-16, 1978.
5. Howard Bowen, *Social Responsibilities of the Businessman* (New York: Harper and Row, 1953).

Bibliography

Adler, Norman A. "The Sounds of Executive Silence," *Harvard Business Review,* July-August 1971.

American Bar Association, *Federal Regulation, Road To Reform,* Commission On Law and the Economy, A.B.A., 1978.

Anderson, James A. "The Potential Impact Of Knowledge Of Market Efficiency On The Legal Liability Of Auditors," *The Accounting Review,* April 1977.

Anderson, Ronald A. *Government and Business,* SouthWestern Publishing Company, New Rochelle, N.Y., 1966.

Armstrong, Robert W. "Why Management Won't Talk," *Public Relations Journal,* November 1970.

Apcar, Leonard M. "Business Backlash—More Companies Bar Regulatory Agencies From Factories, Files," *The Wall Street Journal,* January 19, 1978.

Aronoff, Craig. "Credibility of Public Relations for Journalists," *Public Relations Review,* August 1975.

Banks, Louis. "Memo To The Press: They Hate You Out There," *Atlantic Monthly,* April 1978.

Barnet, Sylvan M. "A Global Look At Advocacy," *Public Relations Journal,* November 1975.

Barry, Charles W. "Letter to the editor," *Cleveland Press,* July 10, 1979.

Becker, Lee B., Raymond A. Martino, and Wayne M. Towers. "Media Advertising Credibility," *Journalism Quarterly,* Summer 1976.

Bernays, Edward L. "The Birth of Public Relations: It Started with Sex," *Management Review,* March 1972.

Blumenthal, W. Michael. "Top Management's Role In Preventing Illegal Payments," *The Conference Board Record,* January-September, 1976.

Bok, Derek. "The President's Report 1977-1978," Harvard University.

Borgida, Chester J. "SEC And The Questionable Payments Controversy," *Public Relations Journal,* April 1977.

Brewster, Arthur J., Herbert H. Palmer, and Robert G. Ingraham. *Introduction To Advertising,* McGraw-Hill, Inc., New York, N.Y., 1954.

Brozen, Yale. "Are New FTC Advertising Policies Inhibiting Competition?" *Journal Of Advertising,* 1973.

Burger, Chester. "How to Meet the Press," *Harvard Business Review,* July-August 1975.

Business Week. "Madison Avenue's Response To Its Critics," June 10, 1972.

——— "A Winning Streak For Business," February 27, 1978.

——— "Government Intervention," April 4, 1977.

——— "The Chilling Impact Of Litigation," June 6, 1977.

——— "The SEC Going Too Far Too Fast?" November 27, 1978.

——— "The Corporate Image: PR To The Rescue," January 22, 1979.

Coe, Ted L., Joshua Ronen, Michael Schiff and George Sorter. *"An Analytical Framework for Materiality Decisions,* Vincent Ross Institute of Accounting Research, New York, June 1976.

Corley, R., R. Black, and O. Reed. *The Legal Environment of Business,* McGraw-Hill, Inc., New York, N.Y., 1963.

Denison, Edward F. "Effects Of Selected Changes In Institutional And Human Environment Upon Output Per Unit Of Input," *Survey Of Current Business,* January 1978.

Dominic, Virgil. *The Cleveland Plain Dealer,* March 8, 1977.

Drucker, Peter. "Good Growth and Bad Growth," *The Wall Street Journal,* April 10, 1979.

Dun's Review. "Business And The Media," May 1977.

Dunfee, T., and F. Gibson. *Modern Business Law,* Grid, Inc., Columbus, Ohio, 1977.

Dunlop, John. "The Limits Of Legal Compulsion," *The Conference Board Record,* March 1976.

Ehrbar, A.F. "The Backlash Against Business Advocacy, *Fortune,* July 1978.

Erickson, M.L., T.W. Dunfee and F.F. Gibson. *Antitrust And Trade Regulation,* Grid, Inc., Columbus, Ohio, 1977.

Flavin, J.B. "The Business/Media Game," *Leaders,* October, November, December, 1978.

Forbes. "You Can't Legislate Accounting Principles," October 2, 1978.

Forbes, Malcolm. "Fact and Comment," *Forbes,* May 28, 1979.

Flom, Joseph H., and Peter A. Atkins. "The Expanding Scope of SEC Disclosure Laws," *Harvard Business Review,* July-August 1974.

Galbraith, John Kenneth. *Economics and The Public Purpose,* Signet and Mentor Books, New York, N.Y., 1975.

Gibson, Martin L. "The Public Thinks We Slant the News," *The Bulletin of the American Society of Newspaper Editors,* September 1972.

Gillis, John G. "Securities Law And Corporate Disclosure," *Financial Analysts Journal,* February 1976.

——— "Securities Law And Regulation," *Financial Analysts Journal,* November 1975.

Goldstein, Tom. "Business and the Law," *The New York Times,* May 19, 1978.

Graham, Katherine. "If 'Business Credibility' Means Anything," *Conference Board Review,* March 1976.

Graham, Katherine. "Business and the Press," *University of Michigan Business Review,* January 1976.

Green, Wayne E. "All-Purpose Panel: Virginia State Corporation Commission Regulates Everything," *The Wall Street Journal,* August 16, 1978.

Grilliot, Howard J. *Introduction to Law and the Legal System,* Houghton Mifflin Co., Boston, Mass., 1979.

Grotta, Gerald L., Earnest Larking, and Bob J. Carrell. "News Vs. Advertising: Does The Audience Perceive the 'Journalistic Distinction'?" *Journalism Quarterly,* Autumn 1976.

Guzzardi, Walter. "A Difference Of Opinion. What the SEC Expects From Corporate Lawyers," *Fortune,* October 23, 1978.

Hakansson, Nils H. "Interim Disclosure And Public Forecasts. An Economic Analysis And Framework For Choice," *The Accounting Review,* April 1977.

Hammond, George. "How Paid Messages Do The Job," *Public Relations Journal,* November 1975.

Hewitt, James O. "Developing Concepts of Materiality and Disclosure," *The Business Lawyer,* April, 1977.

Hill, I. William. "Quality of Business Reporting Discussed at Seminar," *Editor and Publisher,* February 11, 1978.

Holmes, Sandra L. "Executives Should Be Seen And Heard," *Business Horizons,* April, 1977.

Ibrahim, Youssef M. "A.B.A. Unit Urges Less Regulation," *The New York Times,* August 9, 1978.

Jugenheimer, Donald W. "How To Evaluate Corporate Advertising," *Public Relations Journal,* November 1975.

Karr, Albert R., and Leonard M. Apcar, "Car Trouble—Government Pressure Propels Auto Recalls Toward A New High," *The Wall Street Journal,* August 16, 1978.

Kirkpatrick, Miles W. "Advertising and the Federal Trade Commission," *Journal of Advertising,* November 1972.

Koff, Gail J. "Right of Privacy vs. Society's Need To Know," *Public Relations Journal,* October 1975.

Kristol, Irving, "The Underdeveloped Profession," *The Public Interest, no. 6, winter 1967.*

Land, John S. *"Drive To Curb Kickbacks And Bribes By Business,"* U.S. News & World Report, September 4, 1978.

Linowes, David F. "The Right To Be Left Alone," *Business and Society Review,* 1976-1977.

Loevinger, Lee. "The Attack On Advertising and The Goals of Regulations," *Conference Board Record,* January 1973.

Mason, Robert S. "What's a PR Director For, Anyway?" *Harvard Business Review,* September-October 1974.

McCloy, John J. "Improper Payments And The Responsibility Of The Board Of Directors," *Conference Board Record,* January 1976.

―――― McCloy, John J. "American Bar Association Committee on Law and the Economy," *The New York Times,* August 9, 1978.

Mechling, Thomas B. "The Mythical Ethics Of Law, PR and Accounting," *Business and Society Review,* 1976-1977.

Menke, William C. "Marketing And The Federal Trade Commission Act," *Management Review,* September 1975.

Minnesota Law Review, "The Regulation of Corporate Image Advertising," 1974-1975.

Morrow, Lance. "The Politics of the Box Populi", *Time,* June 11, 1979.

Nader, Ralph and Mark Green, "Don't Pay Those High Legal Bills," *The New York Times Magazine,* November 20, 1978.

Nader, Ralph. "The Hidden Executive," *Issues In Business and Society,* edited by George Steiner, Random House, New York, N.Y., 1971.

Nelson, Harold L., and Dwight L. Teeter. *Law of Mass Communications,* The Foundation Press, Inc., Mineola, N.Y. 1969.

New York Times. "Disclosure In Freedom Act Upheld," April 19, 1979.

—— "SEC Head Warns Corporate Lawyers On Ethics, August 9, 1978.

Newton, Lauren K. "Process For Assessing Materiality," *CPA Journal,* May 1977.

O'Toole, John E. "Advocacy Advertising Shows the Flag," *Public Relations Journal,* November 1975.

Otwell, Ralph. "Big, Bad Business in the Hands of the Devil Press," *Quill Magazine,* reprinted in *Media 77-Houston,* by Foundation for American Communications.

Palmer, Jay. "The Rising Risk Of Regulation," *Time* November 27, 1978.

Pastena, Victor, and Joshua Ronen. "Some Hypotheses On The Pattern Of Managements Formal Disclosure." Vincent Ross Institute of Accounting Research, working paper 78-2, July 1978.

Perry, James M. "Jack Anderson Empire Grows—and So Does Criticism it Receives," *Wall Street Journal,* April 25, 1979.

Pitkin, R.B. "An Analysis of the News Media," *American Legion Magazine, March, 1970.*

Pitofsky, Robert. "An FTC View Of Advertising, The Conference Board Record, January 1973.

Posner, Richard A. *Regulation of Advertising By The FTC,* American Enterprise Institute For Public Policy Research, Washington, D.C.

Richter, Robert F. "A Review Of APB Opinion No. 22: Disclosure of Accounting Policies," *CPA Journal,* January 1973.

Robbins, H. Zane. "Your New Quarterly Report," *Public Relations Journal,* April 1976.

Ronen, Joshua. "Information Generation And Disclosure By Corporations," *The Accounting Review,* April 1977.

Rubin, Bernard, editor. *Big Business and Mass Media,* D.C. Heath & Company, Lexington, Mass., 1977.

Rubin, David M. "When The Press Puts Pressure On Business," *Management Review,* February 1973.

Sachs, William S. and Joseph Chasin. "Executives View Corporate Advertising," *Public Relations Journal,* November, 1976.

Schnepper, Jeff A. "The Accountants Liability Under Rule 10b-5 and Section 10(b) of the Securities Exchange Act of 1934: The Hole in Hotchfelder," *The Accounting Review,* July 1977.

Sethi, S. Prakash. "Business and the News Media. The Paradox of Informed Misunderstanding," *California Management Review*, Spring 1977.
——— "Dangers of Advocacy Advertising," *Public Relations Journal*, November, 1976.
——— "Issue-Oriented Corporate Advertising,"*California Management Review*, Fall 1976.
Shaffer, Harold, and Herbert Greenwald. *Independent Retailing*, Prentice Hall, Inc. Englewood Cliffs, N.J., 1976.
Simmons, Steven J. "Commercial Advertising and the Fairness Doctrine: The New F.C.C. Policy in Perspective," *Columbia Law Review*, May-December 1975.
Simon, David H., "You Can't Buy Good Public Relations," *Management Review*, April 1973.
Simon, William. "A Note Of Caution About Business In Politics," *Dun's Review*, April 1979.
Stein, Harry. "How 60 Minutes Makes News," *The New York Times Magazine*, May 6, 1979.
Steiner, George A. *Business and Society*, Random House, New York, N.Y., 1975.
———, editor. *Issues In Business and Society*, Random House, New York, N.Y., 1971.
Steiner, John F. "The Business Response To Public Distrust," *Business Horizons*, April 1979.
Stephenson, Lee. "Prying Open Corporations: Tighter Than Clams," *Business and Society Review*, 1974.
Sterling, Christopher H., and Timothy R. Haight. *The Mass Media: Aspen Institute Guide to Communication Industry Trends*, Praeger Publishers, New York, N.Y., 1978.
Stridsberg, Albert. "How To Organize Controversy Advertising. *Public Relations Journal*, November 1976.
Richter, Robert F. "A Review of APB Opinion No. 22 Disclosure Of Accounting Policies," *The CPA Journal*, January 1973.
Taft, Robert W., and Ann F. Hanby. "Disclosure: Another Busy Year Ahead," *Public Relations Journal*, April 1977.
Tallman, Robert J. "Government and the Advertising Industry," *Journal of Advertising*, November 1972.
Taylor, Arthur R. "Why Business Got A Bad Name." *Business and Society Review*, December 1977.
Thain, Gerald J. "Advertising Regulation: The Contemporary FTC Approach," *Fordham Urban Law Journal*, Vol. 1, 1972-3.
Time. "The Swarming Lobbyists," August 7, 1978.
U.S. News and World Report. "Drive To Curb Kickbacks and Bribes By Business," September 4, 1978.
Ulman, Neil. "Business Lobby Companies Organize Employees and Holders into a Political Force," *The Wall Street Journal*, August 15, 1978.
Wall Street Journal. "EPA To Propose Softening Some Pollution Rules, August 9, 1978.

——— "U.S. Announces New Policy to Encourage Voluntary Disclosure Of Antitrust Acts," October 5, 1978

Walsh, Edward J. "Why the Media Distrust Business," *Cleveland Magazine, September, 1977.*

Washington Star, March 5, 1979.

Ways, Max. "Business Needs To Do A Better Job of Explaining Itself," *Fortune,* September 1972.

Weidenbaum, Murray L. *Business, Government and the Public,* Prentice Hall, Englewood Cliffs, N.J., 1977.

——— *Impacts of Government Regulation,* Center For The Study Of American Business, St. Louis, July 1978.

Weinstein, Edward A. "Disclosure: Too Much Or Too Little?" *CPA Journal,* April 1977.

Westin, Alan F. "Ideas and Trends," *Business Week,* May 14, 1979.

Wiesen, Jeremy L. *Regulating Transactions In Securities,* West Publishing Company, St. Paul, Minn., 1975.

Young, Davis. Speech to IABC Cleveland, Ohio, chapter, Cleveland, Ohio, April, 1979.

Index